Stalking the Story

How to Find Your Screenplay's Story with Help from TV's Greatest Detectives

Jay Douglas

ALPHA

A member of Penguin Group (USA) Inc.

ALPHA BOOKS

Published by the Penguin Group

Penguin Group (USA) Inc., 375 Hudson Street, New York, New York 10014, USA

Penguin Group (Canada), 90 Eglinton Avenue East, Suite 700, Toronto, Ontario M4P 2Y3, Canada (a division of Pearson Penguin Canada Inc.)

Penguin Books Ltd., 80 Strand, London WC2R 0RL, England

Penguin Ireland, 25 St. Stephen's Green, Dublin 2, Ireland (a division of Penguin Books Ltd.)

Penguin Group (Australia), 250 Camberwell Road, Camberwell, Victoria 3124, Australia (a division of Pearson Australia Group Pty. Ltd.)

Penguin Books India Pvt. Ltd., 11 Community Centre, Panchsheel Park, New Delhi—110 017, India

Penguin Group (NZ), 67 Apollo Drive, Rosedale, North Shore, Auckland 1311, New Zealand (a division of Pearson New Zealand Ltd.)

Penguin Books (South Africa) (Pty.) Ltd., 24 Sturdee Avenue, Rosebank, Johannesburg 2196, South Africa

Penguin Books Ltd., Registered Offices: 80 Strand, London WC2R 0RL, England

International Standard Book Number: 978-1-61564-124-6
Library of Congress Catalog Card Number: 2011908148

13   12   11   8   7   6   5   4   3   2   1

Interpretation of the printing code: The rightmost number of the first series of numbers is the year of the book's printing; the rightmost number of the second series of numbers is the number of the book's printing. For example, a printing code of 11-1 shows that the first printing occurred in 2011.

Printed in the United States of America

Note: This publication contains the opinions and ideas of its author. It is intended to provide helpful and informative material on the subject matter covered. It is sold with the understanding that the author and publisher are not engaged in rendering professional services in the book. If the reader requires personal assistance or advice, a competent professional should be consulted.

The author and publisher specifically disclaim any responsibility for any liability, loss, or risk, personal or otherwise, which is incurred as a consequence, directly or indirectly, of the use and application of any of the contents of this book.

Trademarks: All terms mentioned in this book that are known to be or are suspected of being trademarks or service marks have been appropriately capitalized. Alpha Books and Penguin Group (USA) Inc. cannot attest to the accuracy of this information. Use of a term in this book should not be regarded as affecting the validity of any trademark or service mark.

Most Alpha books are available at special quantity discounts for bulk purchases for sales promotions, premiums, fund-raising, or educational use. Special books, or book excerpts, can also be created to fit specific needs.

For details, write: Special Markets, Alpha Books, 375 Hudson Street, New York, NY 10014.

To Peter Falk, who showed us the power of
asking just one more question.
And to Penny, Carol, Mom, and Dad.

Contents

Foreword

"God," the great architect Ludwig Mies once said, "is in the details," and this may very well be true. I would only add that if he is, he's in very good company.

Look closely, and you'll see James Bond in there also. *Casablanca*'s Rick Blaine? Absolutely, along with hundreds of other characters whose personae on film were quickly and memorably defined for us via the precise and telling *detail*.

When Bond steps up to a bar and orders his signature "vodka martini, shaken not stirred," we understand at once that the suave British agent is, first of all, a man's man (he's no teetotaler) and certainly sophisticated (he didn't ask for a Budweiser, did he?), and above all, fastidious (he's very particular about his libations). Five words of dialogue, and we feel as if we know the man. And we do.

By the same token, we understand a good deal of Bogart's Rick Blaine within moments of meeting him in *Casablanca*. Why? Because our first glimpse of the sardonic barkeep shows him knocking back drinks and playing chess *by himself* in a corner of his own bustling café in wartime Morocco.

Do we need Veronica Mars to tell us that Rick is a prosperous, intelligent guy who doesn't much care for the company of others? Of course not. We've inferred this much on our own, thank you. And our knowledge is sweeter because it was inferred.

The cunning screenwriter (which we all aspire to be) forces the audience into constantly making deductions, forcing them to think like a detective.

He tries, whenever possible, to lead them to a conclusion rather than sapping them over the head, tying them up with bailing wire, and driving them there at top speed in the back of a blue sedan.

Consider the old ribald joke about the madam of the, ahem, house of ill repute who answers the front door to find a double-amputee leering up at her. "And just what is it *you* want?" demands the woman, to which the limbless fellow replies, "I rang the doorbell, didn't I?" I warned you. But my point is, this joke derives its power—*all* its power—through implication. By being forced into making certain deductions (*Hang on, how can a guy with no arms or legs* possibly *ring the front door be—ohhhhh!*), we, the audience, are not just passive listeners anymore, but rather active participants in the story, and therefore more invested in the outcome. And we give ourselves a hearty pat on the back for figuring it out.

The old standby is evergreen: whenever possible, show rather than tell, because knowledge *inferred* makes the stronger impression.

But of course, asking the audience to be Adrian Monk means the screenwriter—that is, *you* (always your own first audience)—needs to start playing detective, too. *You're* the one supplying all the crucial little details to make the audience go from passive to active and get them invested in your characters. And in *Stalking the Story,* Jay Douglas has some tips on how to do that—a lot of them.

Jay, in fact, shows you how breaking out the old Deerstalker cap can be a novel and effective way of constructing your entire screenplay. It's an approach I wish I'd come up with.

Indeed, if the idea were mine, I would have probably written the book you are holding instead of merely the foreword. And if my words are making me sound petty, envious, and bitter right now, well ….

Good sleuthing! (You're ready to get started!)

And, of course, happy writing ….

David Breckman
Co-executive producer, *Monk*
August 2011

Introduction

It's the sort of thing that could happen to you. One little word and your whole screenplay—which has been hanging in the balance—tips over onto the wrong side of history. It happened to Elizabeth, an undergrad enrolled in a respected film school in southern California. Elizabeth's script for her screenwriting class was a decent attempt. Act I flew by, and its momentum propelled the screenplay all the way to page 50. Then, thud. Everything stopped. Her classmates knew it. Elizabeth knew it. Try as she might, she couldn't crank up the momentum again.

As the class reviewed her work, Elizabeth's eyes turned to the professor, a Hollywood insider, former development executive, and part-time faculty member. Elizabeth was convinced he would reveal all his secrets and solve all her problems in just a few minutes. After all, he tackled this sort of problem every day in his industry career.

"Put a dead cat in the mailbox," the professor said. The low-level hubbub of students discussing the script halted. The oracle had spoken, and now the students were duty bound to interpret its words. So they did.

"You could kill Amy's mother," said one student.

"Or Amy could get in an accident," said another. From there, interpretations and suggestions piled on each other like cars in a chain-reaction collision.

"Wait," the professor said. "You're complicating things. Just put a dead cat in the mailbox."

What confused the students, who had interpreted the dead cat meta-phorically, and what didn't faze the professor at all, was that the appear-ance of a dead cat had nothing to do with anything in the previous 50 pages. There were no cats, no pets, no pet murders, no cult rituals, no mice problems, not even a visible-from-the-street mailbox to hold the cat in the first place.

The professor was right. Elizabeth's exposition-laden script needed something to get the characters moving again, and the dead cat surely gave them a mystery to dote on. With those seven words, the professor had fixed the script problem … and crippled Elizabeth's project. For the same reasons Elizabeth needed a dead cat on page 50, she also needed one every 10 pages or so.

Long before the landscape was littered with dead felines, Elizabeth had abandoned the script, deciding it was one of those good ideas that just wouldn't work. The tragedy is, her idea was quite workable. Unfortunately, Elizabeth never got the help she needed. The professor had sized up the situation and determined it to be a script problem.

Sadly, Elizabeth didn't have a *script* problem.

She had a *story* problem.

Script versus story. Two little words. Had the professor recognized the difference, Elizabeth might have gone on to finish her script.

Worse yet, Elizabeth had the most common story problem of all: she didn't have one. Her lack of a story was obvious from her first day in class. Asked what her story was about, Elizabeth described it in terms of beats. Amy loses her job. Amy goes to a bar to drown her sorrows. Amy meets a man. The man buys her dinner and offers her a sympathetic ear.

"Yes, Elizabeth, but what's the story about?" said the professor.

"Well, Amy loses her job. She goes to a bar …."

Script versus story. It wasn't only Amy who lost her job—Elizabeth lost hers, too.

This incident happened two decades ago, and I'm still reminded of it every time an agent or producer tells me about the sorry state of the scripts he or she receives from screenwriters:

- There's no story arc.

- The protagonist lacks a strong want or need.

- The protagonist has little or nothing to lose.

- There's no conflict.

"These scripts have problems," they say. I disagree. The scripts are doing exactly what they're supposed to do. They're converting the underlying story into a form that can be rendered on the screen.

The scripts are fine.

The stories are in a world of hurt.

Meanwhile, agents, producers, consultants, executives, professors, friends, parents, spouses, children, cab drivers, baristas, and—*gulp*—authors all offer suggestions that, like Elizabeth's professor, fix the script.

This book is different. We're going to fix your story. In fact, we'll do more than fix it. We'll find it. We'll find the story you want to tell, the one you feel, the one you know it to be—the one you can't quite articulate. We'll find the story that, like Elizabeth, you may only be able to convey through ponderous, interminable beats. Or it may be the one that comes out prematurely and partially formed, much like, "There are these four nurses in a hospital in Boston. They live together. It's hilarious." (I am not making this up. Someone actually pitched this idea to me as a fully formed story.)

This is a true how-to book. It dispenses with the terminology, rules, and conventional wisdom often associated with screenwriting instruction. In this book, I help you find your story by putting you on the trail of the only parties responsible for it—your characters. With the help of this book, you're going to find the story behind your screenplay with some good old-fashioned detective work.

No, I'm not kidding.

Like detective work, developing a story is a matter of asking questions, gathering information, and making choices. Detectives work with real people. Writers work with imaginary characters. Nevertheless, the techniques and results are very much the same.

I've made asking questions and gathering information a regular part of my writing and teaching practices. The methods in this book have helped my students, my friends, and me find the stories we've wanted to tell. They'll do the same for you.

Something drew you to the material you want to turn into a script. Whatever it is—a thought, a phrase, an event, a dream—there's a story in it. You know it. I know it. And in the course of the next 280 pages or so, we're going to find it.

The game's afoot.

JD
Los Angeles
August 2011

How to Use This Book

If there had been a way to record the stories our hunting and gathering ancestors told each other around the campfire, I suspect a goodly share of those tales would resemble our modern-day detective stories.

Whether for bragging rights or entertainment, it's easy to imagine one tribesman after another spinning a yarn about how he started out with just the barest of information—perhaps a footprint or a bent twig—and went on to stalk and bring down the big game. There's something about the hunt for clues—the ingenuity needed to find them, the challenge in putting them together, the craftiness of revealing heretofore unknown secrets—that strikes some primal chord in all of us.

When a writer writes a story, he or she starts with the barest of ideas as to what the story's about. The writer has to follow the characters, figure out what they're doing, piece together all their actions, and cleverly reveal the results. Writers and detectives require many of the same skills and use many of the same techniques. We just don't think of it that way.

In this book, we will.

For the purposes of this book, you're a detective—not just any detective, but a story detective. You've been hired to find out what happened to the hero of your story. Beginning with the smallest clues, you'll investigate the hero's actions as he moves through your story, locate witnesses to his actions, interview the people he encounters, and uncover clues he leaves behind. When you're done, you'll deliver to your clients a short report, which is really a short prose outline of your story, ready to be worked into a screenplay.

Along the way, you'll get help from some of the great television detectives. (You can read their bios online at stalking-the-story.com.) Great is a subjective term. I picked my favorites. Yours may differ. I encourage you to join in the debate at stalking-the-story.com.

Each chapter in the book describes another step in the story detective process, along with tips for carrying out the step and worksheets for uncovering and organizing information. (You can download a complete set of these worksheets at stalking-the-story.com.) In each chapter, I've included examples demonstrating how the steps in the chapter might be applied to a sample story that's developed throughout the book. If the application of a step or the use of a worksheet isn't immediately clear, check the examples for ways of working through things.

The whole process is designed to encourage brainstorming—or what I call brain-sleuthing, a combination of brainstorming and detective work—creativity, and original thinking. As such, feel free to modify any of the methods, tips, and auxiliary material so they work for you. (In fact, if you have ideas for better questions or enhanced worksheets, there's a place on stalking-the-story.com for you to share your ideas with others and pick up new ideas you can use.)

While the idea of playing story detective may sound a little lighthearted, the methods and techniques in this book have proven effective in helping both beginning and advanced screenwriters turn their ideas into stories. What's more, the approach is grounded firmly in narrative theory. Theorists have long understood we become detectives when we read or watch stories unfold. We look for clues as to how the story will develop. We draw conclusions about what's really happened and what will happen next. We try to beat the hero (and the author) to the ending. We're out to "solve" the story before the story ends.

We're detectives when we watch films. Now we'll be detectives when we write them.

If you find something in this book that's not working for you, please take the central idea of each chapter and apply it in the way that makes sense for you. If, in the course of working through a chapter, you suddenly get that flash of insight that tells you exactly what the next step in your story is, stop right there and write it down. The objective of each chapter is to help you inch closer to that all-important story outline. Each chapter is a guide and source of inspiration, but it's not a substitute for your own instincts and creativity.

As you work through the chapters, write down how you've improved upon my suggestions. Then, visit stalking-the-story.com and share your ideas with your fellow story detectives. If at any time you find yourself stuck—if the material in this book isn't working for you—that's another reason to visit the website.

Someone may have posted just the tip you need to get going again.

Acknowledgments

According to conventional wisdom, no one reads the acknowledgments unless they think their name's in there.

Yet here we are.

I suspect you're one of the millions of people not mentioned here, so I imagine you're curious to see whether any famous people were involved in creating this book. Well, yes and no.

There's Danny Simon, one of the fathers of the American television sitcom and brother of playwright Neil Simon. Years ago Danny said to me, "The more you know, the more you can write." Danny's no longer with us to see what his words morphed into, but without him, you'd be holding a vastly different book in your hands.

There's my wife, Penny, who is famous in education circles for her work in helping inner-city youths get college educations. Around the Douglas household, she's famous for making sure I get out of bed and into my office every morning, and for urging me to write yet another book when she knew full well how unpleasant I become on those days when my writing expectations aren't met.

Then there's my friend and confidant, Jack Gostl, who is famous if you're in the mutual funds business and need specialized computer software; Jeffrey Davis, who used to write for *Love Boat;* Greg Dean, the dean of stand-up comedy teachers; writer Shirl Hendryx, who knew most of the television detectives mentioned in this book personally; David Breckman of *Monk* and *Saturday Night Live* writing fame; Steven Bolson, the famous screenwriter, just not yet; Bill Gladstone, a familiar name in literary agent and author circles and my agent at Waterside Productions; and Kathleen Rushall, who's not nearly as famous as she ought to be.

Many other people have toiled on this book in relative obscurity, and they deserve their moment of fame. I'm talking about the editorial and production staff at Alpha Books, who somehow know how to turn every bump in the road into a smooth stretch of highway when taking words from a file to ink on paper. Special thanks to Lori Hand, Christy Wagner, Kayla Dugger, Christy Hackerd, John Etchison, and Brian Massey.

Once again, this is a book that never would have happened without the encouragement and support of my editor, Randy Ladenheim-Gil, who's very well known among people who know her.

There are many other famous people whose names are not mentioned here but whose contributions to this book, both directly and indirectly, cannot be overstated. As the author, I had the pleasure of incorporating their ideas and insights. If this book helps you, please contact me at pagingDrDoug.com/contact, and I'll be sure your comments are distributed to all those responsible.

As always, mistakes, shortcomings, errors, omissions, and anything you find downright unhelpful stop squarely with me. I need to hear about them so I can do better next time.

Thanks, too, to all my screenwriting students at Loyola Marymount University, who were not only the best sounding boards for my ideas, but also who provided me with endless hours of entertainment through their scripts and classroom banter. Semester after semester, they reminded me that one obligation of all writers is to pass on to future writers the unbounded exhilaration and endless joys of our craft.

And hope they never find out otherwise.

Prologue

A piece of advice: never, ever ask "What is a story?" at a convention of literary and narrative theorists. (Or ask it only if you have nothing more pressing to do, such as trimming your toenails.) If 50 theorists are in the room, you'll get 337 different opinions.

And that's before they start bickering.

The world doesn't need opinion number 338, so I'll stick with one that's worked well for my students and colleagues, and follow E. M. Forster's lead:

> A story is a collection of events linked by cause and effect.

(Forster's example, which comes in many different flavors, goes something like this. "The king died and then the queen died" is a chronology because it merely positions the events in time. The king died before the queen. "The king died and then the queen died of grief" is a story because the queen's death, the effect, was caused by the king's death.)

As it turns out, the mechanics of storytelling are pretty straightforward. Out of all the events that happen to the subject of your story, select the ones you need. Once you've selected them, order them in the way you want the story to unwind. Then, tell your story.

Select. Order. Tell.

Thanks to Forster, we know just what events to select. We select the events linked by cause and effect. If you're telling a story about a guy who goes back in time to foil a plot to destroy the world, you probably don't need to include his daily breakfast routine or how much he likes his grandmother's pot roast.

What, though, are the events that make up the story? It's well and good that we include only those linked by cause and effect, but that bit of wisdom does little to tell us what events we're linking and how to find them. At this point, the story detective's work begins. To understand the role of the story detective, think about your family.

Every family, in every generation, has a colorful relative—even if that color is black, as in black sheep. Let's assume you have two such colorful relations, Uncle Horace and Aunt Francine.

They rob banks.

Aunt Francine, who jumped the middle-age shark years ago, still cuts quite a figure. She walks into a bank, opens up her cloth overcoat, and stands there stark naked. While everyone stares (*marvels* would be the word she'd choose), Uncle Horace leaps out from behind a potted plant with gun in hand and then loots the till. Witness reports are sketchy— Uncle Horace wears a Donald Duck mask, and no one is able to describe Aunt Francine north of her breastbone—and the duo has pulled off enough heists to buy a beachfront villa in a wonderful country called No Extradition Treaty.

You've decided their lives and times would make a riveting (and profitable) documentary. At the time, they were the darlings of America's mid-level hoodlum set. Horace and Francine don't have e-mail and they've canceled their Facebook pages, so you can't talk to them personally, but you know your documentary has to answer important questions: Why did they do it? How'd they get away with it? Who were their biggest allies and adversaries?

Where do you begin?

Chances are, you start by interviewing people in your family because you have easy and unlimited access to them. Then, you widen the circle to friends and neighbors, bank customers and employees, the police detectives who investigated the crimes, Aunt Francine's hair stylist, Uncle Horace's chiropractor, and acquaintances who shared your aunt's and uncle's hospitality in their beachfront villa. You might walk in their tracks by visiting some of the banks they robbed, reading stories in newspaper morgues and online, looking through television news footage, and combing YouTube.

Whether you call this research, background information collecting, or just plain fact gathering, you need to collect all the necessary details before you can piece together your documentary—before you can decide what's important and what's not, what opens the film, and what brings it to a close. What you're doing is no different from what the police detectives did while tracking down Horace and Francine. The only difference is the objective: a police detective is out to bring them to justice; you're out to tell their story on film. If the case is still active, you might bump into a detective or two in your work. You might even become buddies, joined by the commonality of your occupations.

What makes your jobs possible, the detective and the documentarian, is that the information you both need already exists. Just by living out their lives, Uncle Horace and Aunt Francine left marks of their existence across the years—a breadcrumb trail of clues. You and the police detective need to find and follow those clues, because only then can you answer the questions you posed at the start of your project, and only then can you decide how to put together a case or a documentary.

What if you want to make a film about Uncle Horace and Aunt Francine and the two of them aren't your relatives but products of your imagination? That seems like a different story (no pun intended), doesn't it? Uncle Horace and Aunt Francine don't exist. There are no breadcrumbs to follow. You have to scatter them yourself. Heck, you have to bake them and grind them up first. When you sit down to write, there's nothing to work with, no trail to follow, no accomplices to interview, no Google searches, and no snarky remarks from Mom about how Horace was never good enough for her sister.

What if there were? What if there were a trail? Then you'd be back in detective mode.

One way of thinking about your job of finding the story behind your screenplay is imagining that the characters in your story are real, and that you're a story detective whose job it is to find out what the characters did. To dig up that information, you can use the same techniques you'd apply if these were real people and you were out to tell a true story. Once you know what happened to these characters, you can do just what you'd do if you were making a documentary: interview, examine, and conclude.

When you're done with this book, you'll know as much about the lives of your characters as you would if you were making a documentary about real people. You'll know what they did, where they did it, and why. You'll know who helped them and who stood in their way. You'll see what events you want to select for your story, how they're linked by cause and effect, and how you want to arrange these events in your story's time line.

Then, you'll prepare a short report of your detective work, an outline of your story you can use to fashion the scenes, descriptions, and dialogue of your screenplay.

Uncle Horace and Aunt Francine would be so proud to have such a clever niece or nephew.

Part 1

The Client

Chapter 1

The Case of the Simple Human Truth

It's tough being a story detective.

Hang around the racket long enough, and you learn nothing's ever as it seems. It's like House says, "Everybody lies."

House would be Greg House, M.D., although few story detectives are fooled by the initials after his name. When it comes to detective work, maybe a House isn't a Holmes, but he's got more in common with Sherlock than the matching street numbers on their front doors. House knows the truth isn't in what people tell you but in what they don't talk about. What nobody talks about. What you have to find out for yourself.

People lie, House would tell you. Your case is a case in point.

Detectives invent colorful names for their capers, such as "The Case of the Runaway Monkey," or "The Case of the Crying Class Clown." Spend your days with enough cases, though, and you discover just about every story could be titled "The Case of the Simple Human Truth." All those cases were about lessons or morals you've heard all your life. Crime doesn't pay. Honesty is the best policy. If it's too good to be true, it isn't. Faith in yourself will pull you through.

Whatever it is that made this story start the voices in your head pestering you to death about it, whatever that is, at its heart, is a Simple Human Truth. When you think your story is going south—and it will more times than House diagnoses lupus—what will keep you going is knowing you're really on the trail of a Simple Human Truth.

Think of it as compensation for the hard work ahead.

Over the course of stalking your story, characters, locales, motives, and ideas may come and go. Through it all, the one constant will be that Simple Human Truth. That Simple Human Truth is the reason you took on this case, the reason it's important to you.

That's reason enough to write it down.

Take 5 minutes and make a list of any and all Simple Human Truths that might apply to your story. Write in the margins, on a scrap of paper, a napkin, the palm of your hand, or the soles of your feet—anyplace that lets those voices in your head know you're taking them seriously.

MY SIMPLE HUMAN TRUTH IS IN HERE

Finished? Would House be finished looking for the truth? House, the guy who put a patient's life in danger trying to find out what killed another patient he cared for 20 years earlier?

OR HERE

House once solved a case by having his team tear apart an apartment looking for termites. That's a good enough reason to look behind the walls for your Simple Human Truth.

OR MAYBE HERE

Simple, right? There's the Simple Human Truth you're looking for. It's just hidden, playing peek-a-boo in the paperwork, like everything else in the story detective game. Anyone who thinks this is a glamorous profession, filled with fast cars and faster women, doesn't sit behind a desk, polishing that scuff out of his shoes, all the while dodging paperwork on the one hand and the bill collector on the other. Sometimes, to satisfy one, you have to tackle the other. So put down the shoe polish, and polish off the paperwork.

Read through your list, and underline the three Simple Human Truths you feel will keep you going when those shoes you're polishing clamp down on your feet like a leather vise.

Out of those three, circle the best one, the one that reaches out and grabs hold of you tighter than those shoes.

Every now and again, when your parents call asking you what they did wrong because you didn't become a doctor, look at your Simple Human Truth and remind yourself that tracking down Simple Human Truths is as noble as taking out tonsils.

People lie, House will remind you. Stories (and their detectives) don't.

EXAMPLE

Throughout the book, we'll develop a story based on Uncle Horace and Aunt Francine, the two bank robbers I used in the prologue as an example of real versus imaginary characters. This starting point isn't a story at all. Rather, it's an idea—a curiosity. What if two not-quite-but-almost senior citizens robbed banks? And what if, in the process, they broke most, or all, of the rules of bank robbing? Let's see where these questions lead us, and why.

We begin with a list of possible Simple Human Truths this story could embody.

As a story detective, you'll routinely embark on brain-sleuthing, a combination of brainstorming and detective work. Often, doing so means making lots of lists. Here are some guidelines my students and colleagues have found effective when brain-sleuthing calls for list-making:

- Write quickly.
- Keep writing. Staring into space, daydreaming, pondering, embellishing—in fact, thinking of any kind—is a no-no.
- If it's in your head, put it on your list—no editing allowed.
- If it's on your list, it stays there—no erasing, no deleting, and no crossing out.
- Duplicate ideas, worded differently, are not only allowed, they're encouraged.

MY SIMPLE HUMAN TRUTH IS IN HERE

You're as young as you feel.

Crime does pay.

It doesn't matter what you're doing, as long as you're having fun.

Love will always get you through.

Crime doesn't pay.

He/she who laughs last, laughs best.

Everybody needs somebody.

All's well that ends well.

Honesty is the best policy.

Life begins at 50 (or 60).

It's okay to be silly.

You have to act your age.

You don't have to act your age.

Acting your age is for old people.

Love what you do.

Do what you love.

The secret to a long life is doing what you love.

Who cares what other people say?

There are already some four-star platitudes on the list, some old sayings, some repeats, and a few opposing ideas. All of them are top-of-the-head responses. Let's try for some middle-of-the-head ideas.

OR HERE

We all want to leave a legacy.

Fame is the name of the game.

Everybody's good at something.

You can't take it with you.

You can take it with you.

Here, the list has taken a different tack. The previous ideas centered on age, doing what you love, and being the odd person out (as might befit the black sheep of the family). This second push brings something new to the surface: the idea of leaving something behind that's bigger than yourself, the notion that what you do can live on.

You might also call making lists, and other brain-sleuthing activities, "The Case of the Low-Hanging Fruit." The obvious ideas, the ones that are easiest to reach, come out first. The really creative ideas, the ones that amaze even you, take a second (or third) effort. There will be times when you'll ask yourself, *What makes my story unique? I've heard all this before.* The answer is, in part, the hard-to-reach fruit. Let's see if we can squeeze out one more Simple Human Truth.

OR MAYBE HERE

It's never too late to make your mark.

Perhaps expectedly, that final push resulted in an idea that combines other ideas on the list. Still, it's an interesting thought not quite expressed by any single previous one.

We need three ideas for the bonus round. Let's try (in no particular order):

Life begins at 50 (or 60).

It's never too late to make your mark.

Fame is the name of the game.

There's no right or wrong here. These three seem to encapsulate the theme running through the list: age versus youth and legacy. There's another theme, that one should love what one does, but age versus youth and fame/legacy seem to be pervasive in society today. Perhaps that's why they've percolated to the top.

Now comes the hard part. Well, not really the hard part, but it seems that way. We need to pick one idea. Writing is all about making choices, and choices are difficult because we never have enough information to make the "right" one. Fortunately, in writing, we don't have to.

If your chosen Simple Human Truth (or any choice, for that matter) doesn't seem to be working, back up and choose again. All choices are tentative when it comes to writing. Keep the ones that work for you and fix the ones that don't. With that in mind, let's try …

It's never too late to make your mark.

… as the Simple Human Truth at the heart of this story. The statement seems to capture notions in people's minds these days—we all deserve our 15 minutes of fame, aging baby boomers aren't going to observe tradition and quietly step aside for the generations behind them, and humans want to know they'll be remembered after they're gone.

It's never too late to make your mark.

Let's see how Horace and Francine make a case for that.

Chapter 2

The Case of the Cacophony of Voices

It's one of those days story detectives have too many of. The hours are counting down while the bills are piling up. When there aren't any stories, there's not much for a story detective to do. While you're wondering if it's just you or if the office walls really are closing in, you can't help but notice the loud ringing coming from your telephone.

"Get that for me will you, doll?" you say, forgetting for the moment that you don't have a secretary—not to mention the fact that she'd probably give you that nose job you never wanted if you called her "doll." By the time you answer the phone, the voices at the other end seem lost in their own conversation. Conversation? A barroom brawl in three-part harmony is more like it. The only word you can make out clearly is "HELP."

From what you can glean from the gaggle of voices competing for your attention, the hero of a story has disappeared. "Certain friends and acquaintances" have "certain vested interests" in finding out where the hero is and exactly what happened to him. It seems the hero had "a problem of a personal nature," and he may have taken "certain steps toward fixing said problem." The "certain friends and acquaintances" are concerned that what the hero learned "on account of said steps" might have changed the hero in "certain ways that may have contributed to the hero's current condition of unavailability."

The voices go on to tell you they're authorized to offer you "a certain remuneration that will be commensurate with results—one way or the other." Considering the current demands on your time, you can say this case will receive your full attention.

As much as the call raised your spirits, you have to admit the cacophony of voices all clamoring for attention has all the charm of the floor of the Stock Exchange during a market crash—and is reminiscent of the voices you hear in your head on those days you think you might be on the trail of a story. Those voices are the ones that got you into the story detective business. You don't bring them up in polite conversation for fear they may be your ticket out of this place and into one of those rooms with padded walls and snug-fitting jackets with wrap-around sleeves.

You catch every fifth word or so, not that you're keeping count. Mostly what you hear is "hero has a problem," "did this," "learned …," "trouble …." If there's a story in there, you can't find it. You need more to go on than words plucked from a dime-store novel.

You need Peggy.

Peggy was Joe Mannix's secretary. Mannix—now there is a detective's detective. Square jawed. Handsome. A hit with the ladies. Tough. Nasty right hook. A hit with the ladies. Honest. Loyal. Smart. Determined. A hit with the ladies.

And he's lost without Peggy.

Calling Peggy a secretary is like calling a secretary a "doll." Only messing with Peggy was likely to get you a tap on the jaw from Mannix's right fist.

Peggy kept Mannix on the foursquare by sitting him down and laying it all out for him. Without Peggy, Mannix might have gone from corporate security to his own private investigating business and back in less time than it takes your girlfriend to spend your weekly profits—when there are any. Not that Mannix always took Peggy's advice—but he seemed to enjoy apologizing to her when he didn't.

The first thing Peggy would do if she were standing in front of you would be to tell you to get your feet off your desk. The second thing she'd do would be to call your attention to the dust your feet kicked up. Then she'd take out her stenographer's pad and start making sense of the gibberish you heard on the phone. You'd talk, she'd scribble, and then hand you something that read …

PEGGY'S NOTE

This is a story about a(n) _____ hero who

_____. The hero _____, and

as a result, learns or discovers _____.

Peggy had a way of cutting right to the quick. She probably could have filled in the blanks and handed you your case in a pair of sentences. But your feet are still on the desk, and the role of Peggy is being played by the face that stares back at you from the mirror every morning.

You can still hear the voices in your head. What are they telling you about the hero? That would probably be Peggy's first question. It's something short—a one- or two-word description that Mannix would appreciate. (As a detective's detective, he was a man of few words.) What do you hear? Brave? Stupid? Arrogant? Foolhardy? Determined? Lonely? Adventurous? Ignored? Slimy? Set in his ways? Honest to a fault?

Like Peggy, you start your own note.

This is a story about a(n) _____ hero

You can hear the voices again. This hero's having a problem. You've seen enough problems and heroes to know it's no stretch imagining the problem is related to the kind of person the hero is. There was that cranky hero who turned his neighbor into an enemy. That honest-to-a-fault hero who was mistaken for a gangster when he returned a bag of money that fell from an armored car. And how about that adventurous hero who couldn't rest until he explored the River of Death?

There's a hero with a problem for every light on Broadway, you think, being too tired to come up with your own analogy. If Peggy were there, she'd tell you it's time to figure out what this hero's problem is. She has a young son, Toby, at home, and spending all night listening to you crib song lyrics isn't what either of them had in mind.

hero who _____.

You don't need Peggy to tell you that if the hero has a problem, he's going to do something about it—maybe even something smart. Or he may do something that keeps lawyers and undertakers in Beamers and Benzes. The cranky hero declares all-out war on his neighbor. The honest hero decides that if he's going to be treated like a gangster, he might as well become one. Or the adventurous hero pinches his wife's winning lottery ticket and sets off down the River of Death (perhaps more of a case for the undertaker than a story detective).

As sure as gin follows tonic, the hero in your case did something about his problem, too.

The hero _____

On any other night, you'd call it a day. You've got a hero with a problem, and he did something about it. You're tired of listening to all those voices, and what you've got now seems like enough to go on. But you had to get Peggy involved, and she's tapping her foot about now, giving you the look your third-grade teacher gave you when you forgot the answer to 2 plus 2.

Granted, you're no Einstein (Peggy would say you're not even a Mannix), but you do remember that 2 plus 2 equals 4, and that for every action, there's some reaction. If the hero did something about his problem, there must have been a result. That's why the "certain friends and acquaintances" are concerned about his "availability." He's a changed man. The hero could be standing right there in front of them, and they might not even realize it. He learned a lesson—maybe something he didn't want to know.

The cranky hero learns to be tolerant of others. The honest hero discovers he was right all along, that honesty is the best policy. The adventurous hero learns it's time to grow up and accept his responsibilities as a family man—right after his wife unlocks the door to the doghouse.

You recall the voices once again. How did the hero change?

and as a result, learns or discovers _____

_____.

This is what those "certain friends and acquaintances" want to know. This is what's going to get you a deposit slip for the "remuneration commensurate with results."

You sit down at your desk to read your note, but is that what Peggy would want you to do?

"Aren't you forgetting something?" Peggy would say. "You can't just tell people like these, 'Everything is okay.' You need proof."

You know what she means. Those "certain friends and acquaintances" aren't about to take your word for an answer. Sooner or later you'll have to show them evidence that the hero is not the same guy they've grown to know and love. What will that be? It's got to be more than a slap on the back and a lunch invitation. "It will have to be something they can see," Peggy would say.

How can you prove to those "certain friends and acquaintances" that when you say the hero's changed you're on the up and up? What can you show them?

PROOF

SOME WAYS WE CAN PROVE THE HERO'S CHANGED

SOME MORE WAYS

AND EVEN A FEW MORE

What are the top three pieces of proof you think will earn you that "remuneration commensurate with results"? Of those three, what's your best choice?

And we know this because _____

_____

_____.

Now you can get to your note.

It has the comfortable familiarity of a pair of old slippers. A hero of a particular personality attempts to solve a problem—most likely one of his own making—in his own particular way, only to learn a lesson that leaves him changed.

It's not much to go on, but Mannix and Peggy have gotten started on less and it's more than you had before.

And besides, there are still those "certain consequences" mentioned in the phone call ….

As the clock ticks toward tomorrow, you just might find that your office is getting larger again. "Thanks, Peggy," you say, even though she isn't really there. Just as well. If she were, she'd probably wonder why you were talking to yourself, or what kind of person spends his days with imaginary characters and gets away with it.

Maybe, you think, *that dry patch is ending.* Of course, that all depends on how much luck you have filling in between the lines of that little piece of prose on your desk.

Then again, luck has nothing to do with it.

Then again, oh yes it does.

But that's a problem for tomorrow.

EXAMPLE

The story seems to be about two people, Horace and Francine. It's not impossible to write a story in which two people make up one hero, but it can be a challenge. Because the job of the hero is to drive the story forward, most of the time one character takes the lead. Let's pick one and make the other a close-second hero.

Picking Horace might be the obvious choice. Choosing Francine might take the story on an unexpected path. In film, bank robberies always seem to be engineered by men. We'll start with her, and if down the line Horace winds up taking over the story, we'll make a hero swap. Right now, it's important we make a choice and get started.

The Simple Human Truth of this story is that you're never too old to leave your mark. Francine, then, is probably feeling old, past her prime, out of the loop, and ordinary. The end of her life is closing in on her, and she feels she has nothing to show for it. In her mind, she's a failure, and it frightens her that she may die that way.

This is a story about a(n) __frightened__ *hero*

Francine has a problem. She's afraid she'll die a failure. That's a workable situation. We can see how someone who believes she's a failure and doesn't want to die that way may want to take steps to change what she sees as the inevitable outcome.

We could ask ourselves what Francine thinks she's a failure at and use that as our problem. Certainly, we want Francine doing something more substantial than wandering through the story bemoaning the fact she's a worthless soul. At this point, though, keeping the situation a little loose can work to our advantage. When we know a little more about Francine, we might discover deeper reasons for her sense of failure than we can come up with now. That Francine doesn't want to die a failure is good enough to begin with.

This is a story about a(n) __frightened__ *hero who* __doesn't want to die a failure__ .

We already know what Francine does about her fear. She enlists the aid of her husband, Horace, and together they rob banks. There are other choices Francine might have made. Given her figure, she might have auditioned for *Dancing with the Stars* or grabbed a feather boa and headed off for *America's Got Talent*. But robbing banks is what got us started on the story of Horace and Francine in the first place, so let's stick with it.

This is a story about a(n) __frightened__ *hero who* __doesn't want to die a failure__ . *The hero* __robs banks with the help of her husband__ .

What does Francine learn or discover as a result of her bank-robbing spree? Once again, we find ourselves overwhelmed by choices. Francine could have learned anything from being frightened is a silly way to live your life to leaving your mark can also mean having a husband who believes in you and is willing to do anything for you.

When we think about the hero changing, though, a good ending place is 180 degrees from where the hero started off. The hero can't change any more than that. Maybe a complete reversal would prove too dramatic or unbelievable given the hero's character. If so, we'll find that out as we follow the hero through the story. Making choices is what we story detectives and writers do, so let's go to the extreme. Francine starts out frightened because she thinks she's an ordinary person who started out life as just a birth statistic and will wind up as nothing more than a one-paragraph obituary. What she learns is that her life matters.

Again, we'll answer how it matters to whom and why as we stalk Francine. At least now we know what signs to look for along the way.

This is a story about a(n) __frightened__ hero who __doesn't want to die a failure__. The hero __robs banks with the help of her husband__, and as a result, learns or discovers __her life matters__.

At the end of the story, how will we know that Francine knows that her life matters? More important, how will we show it? It's not enough for Francine to know it inside. We have to be able to share her feelings with the outside world. Nor is it enough for Francine to tell us how she feels. Maybe Francine is merely saying what she thinks those around her want to hear. What we need is proof that Francine has made her mark and that her life matters. We need something tangible, something we can see.

PROOF

SOME WAYS WE CAN PROVE THE HERO'S CHANGED

She has lots of money in the bank

She's written up in the newspaper

She appears on "The Tonight Show"

People recognize her when she walks down the street

People recognize her name

SOME MORE WAYS

She has her own television show

She has her own cable television network

People imitate her style of dress

People imitate her hair style

AND EVEN A FEW MORE

She has a school named after her

She has a press agent

Francine wants to make her mark, and that's a goal we typically associate with being famous. It's not surprising that the list reflects that. There are some interesting entries, including her having a press agent, that speak to what society considers the trappings of fame. Our job, though, is to find something that combines fame and Francine. What might satisfy her?

The first idea that comes to mind is having money in the bank. Francine isn't poor, but if she and Horace will be robbing banks we can conclude they aren't awash in cash. While money and fame are often linked, we'd have a hard time showing "money in the bank." We could always have Francine hold up a bank statement, or read her balance from a computer screen, but neither of those sounds like an interesting image.

Showing Francine on television, as a guest, a host, or a cable television magnate is far more visual. Our image of Francine, though, is of a rather plain person from a plain background. That's not to say ordinary people can't scale extraordinary heights, only that Francine doesn't seem like she'd be comfortable on television. Nor does it feel right that Francine would be a trendsetter, one of the beautiful people whose every move is watched lest we miss out on some new fad.

Having a school named after her, or having instant face and name recognition—those sound somewhat smaller, more personal, and more aligned with who Francine is. As we will do many times when faced with roughly equal choices, we make one and see where it takes us.

And we know this because <u>people will recognize Francine's face</u>
<u>and name</u> .

It may not look like much, but all the story building blocks are there. We have a hero, the hero has a problem, the problem causes the hero to take an action, and the action has consequences that change the hero.

Chapter 3

The Case of the Persistent Past

Being a story detective may not get you chased by rich dames or slick-haired sharpies with investment deals, but it's the kind of job that, every once in a while, lets you get a good night's sleep. On the other hand, being the hero in a story is the kind of job you wouldn't wish on anybody, not even the newlyweds next door with the bed that creaked right through last night's beauty rest. Bad things happen to heroes.

Heroes are always under pressure. Their lives are filled with ambiguity. They're constantly confronted with failure. Their problems compound regularly. They have to make decision after decision. Half the time they're tired, the other half they're exhausted. Anxiety is their middle name. If they're not anxious, they're frustrated. If they're not frustrated, they're disappointed. Their lives are one part conflict and two parts more conflict. Their relationships last about as long as a piece of litter in Disneyland.

If that's not enough, a good hero's got to dress up in his vulnerabilities, bad habits, and fears and wear them around like an ill-fitting leisure suit. Odds are, if a hero could do anything but be a hero, he'd be out scraping sewer pipes or pushing pickup trucks uphill.

But your job isn't to psychoanalyze heroes, it's to find them, and to do that, you need to know how they've handled their problems in the past. A man reaches his sexual peak at 18 and his physical peak at 22, but everything else is pretty much locked in before the peach fuzz appears on his upper lip. A hero who threw temper tantrums when he was 5 will throw them at 35. Sure, he may not pound on the carpet and hold his breath until he turns blue, but that quiet little kid, who tossed obstacles aside like so much salt over his shoulder before retiring to his room and tearing up his comic books, is today's hero who laughs in the face of adversity and then squeezes himself into a bottle of scotch.

The secret to finding out where the hero is going is backing up over his tracks and finding out where he's been. That's why every detective, if he's lucky, gets to turn to his assistant and say, "Find out everything you can about that guy." If he's not lucky, he's still waiting on that assistant and has to do all the background work himself.

If you're going to do your own digging, you could do a lot worse than follow Jim Rockford's lead. Rockford, the laid-back private investigator who's part ex-con and part con man. He'll be the first to tell you everybody's got secrets. And he doesn't mean the couple of hundred bucks he hides on the bottom of his desk drawer so his father won't find them. Rockford knows that what makes people tick is what those people overlook accidentally on purpose—like the Vietnamese woman who hired him to find her missing brother but neglected to mention it wasn't merely a case of his getting on the wrong bus. It's never a question of whether you'll have to check out the past, but how far back you have to dredge.

It's a little early for dredging, which is definitely a post-lunch occupation, especially after enduring 1,214 bed creaks last night—not that anybody was counting. Besides, your desk feels pretty comfortable beneath your feet. It seems like a good time to figure out just who can sort fact from the hero's fancy.

Parents or foster parents are always good, and so are friends from high school and college—especially if they're holding a grudge. Don't forget the relatives. Not all of them—just the one or two who have a score to settle with the hero's parents. They usually come up with a tidbit or two Mommy and Daddy like to gloss over. Then there are the neighbors. They can be the best. A tiff over the family dog digging up rose bushes can turn into pages of juicy background info you couldn't unearth if your last name were Google. Old bosses and co-workers are good for dredging, too—especially the co-workers. Bosses tend to be afraid of lawsuits, but co-workers just tend to be afraid of being left out.

HERO INTERVIEWEE LIST

USUAL SUSPECTS

NOT-SO-USUAL SUSPECTS

Even through those sleep-deprived eyes you can see you've got quite a list. Everybody you need to …

You catch yourself in mid-thought. You can almost see Rockford, rolling his eyes. Your list is nothing better than a hasty collection of notes written by a guy anxious to get started on a fishing vacation, something Rockford knows like the fins on a rainbow trout. Where's the fact that the naïve Vietnamese client's broken English is all an act? Or that her missing brother worked at an American ranger camp in Vietnam? Or that this nice refugee family is caught up in a black-market smuggling scheme involving half a million American dollars?

The only way you're going to get Rockford to take you seriously is by digging for not-so-usual information from not-so-usual suspects. Look for the kid in the schoolyard who used to sell weed to the hero. The priest who heard his first confession. The hero's current mistress—and her boyfriend.

Suddenly, the desk under your feet doesn't feel all that comfortable. You swing your legs onto the floor, grab your list, and start again.

MORE NOT-SO-USUAL SUSPECTS

One more look at Rockford. Sure, he's still rolling his eyes, but you've got plenty of time to add more names to the list. One glance at Rockford's case files ought to be enough to convince you, and him, that facts don't arrive on schedule or in neat packages. Look at how long it took HIM to find out the client's brother wasn't a spy—the proof was he liked cowboy movies. Story detectives need patience … and sleep. Tomorrow will be a busy day.

The past is about to begin.

We need information about Horace as well as Francine because it appears Horace is almost as important as his wife in this story. We can get specifics on him later, though, when we ask around about the people close to Francine. For now, we'll stick with the people in Francine's background, knowing that some of them may overlap when we check into Horace.

What do we need to know about Francine? Certainly, we need general information such as where she was born, where she lived growing up, and how she met Horace, but it's crucial to know why failure, or not being a failure, is so important to her. Also, she seems pretty proud of her physical condition. Is this pride something recent or something she has possessed most of her life?

Then there's the whole business of robbing banks. It seems like an extreme response to whatever problem she wants to solve. Surely, we need a sense of how she handled frustration and disappointment while growing up. Was bank robbing a spur-of-the-moment solution or something she thought about for months (or years)? Is she methodical or impulsive?

We're not looking for the answers to these questions right now. We're looking for people in Francine's life who could answer them. Let's begin with, in no particular order, the usual suspects. They're the easiest ones, and they may give us clues to the not-so-usual suspects later on.

USUAL SUSPECTS

Mother

Father

Aunt/mother's sister

Sister/younger

Brother/older

Grandfather/maternal

Grandmother/maternal

Best friend growing up

Mother of best friend growing up

Fourth-grade teacher

Soft-serve ice-cream store manager/boss

Childhood next-door neighbor

Current next-door neighbor

Boss at last job

Administrative assistant at last job

Computer tech at last job

Co-worker with crush on her

As we choose people to interview, we're simultaneously making decisions about Francine's early years. Her first job was at a soft-serve ice-cream store. She has or had a best friend. Something significant happened in fourth grade that we'll hear about from her teacher. Making these choices is part of the brain-sleuthing process, and it's important to go with your instincts. Fourth grade popped up for a reason, even if we don't know what that is right now. Whether or not we interview every person on the list, just their presence helps describe and define Francine's life. The more people on the list, the more clearly we can picture who Francine is.

The same rules apply to the not-so-usual suspects. The people we add to the list, no matter how offbeat, contribute to the profile we're building of our hero.

If you feel stuck, consider the people in your own life who know the most about you. Who are the people you confided in or who are in a position to watch you or hear things about you? With whom did you have run-ins over the years? Does Francine have the same or similar people in her life? If so, put them on the list.

NOT-SO-USUAL SUSPECTS

Hair stylist

Mail carrier

Supermarket checker

Middle-school bully

Salesman who sold Francine her first new car

Gynecologist

Woman she rear-ended in auto accident

Kid from down the block

Adding people from her "last" job to the list implies Francine doesn't have a current job. A middle-school bully conjures up images of a school life that didn't fit the Norman Rockwell mold. For many people, a first car is a major life event. It may be interesting to see how Francine handled it. (That the salesman sold *her* the car also implies that she might not have been married at the time.)

Now that we have an idea of who's on the investigative radar, we can focus on who can help us prepare a dossier of Francine's life before the story begins. We can use the dossier to predict her life as the story unfolds.

Chapter 4

The Case of the Celebrated Story

Hang around the story detective racket long enough, and you get to follow heroes to some pretty impressive places—Yosemite National Park, the Chicago lakefront, the Swiss Alps. Of course, you get your share of bar basements, sewer plants, and meat lockers, too. Hang around the racket even longer, and you start noticing all these places remind you of one thing.

Pieces in a jigsaw puzzle.

Not your standard got-it-for-a-birthday-gift-five-years-ago-and-haven't-gotten-around-to-opening-the-box puzzle. It's the kind of jigsaw puzzle that's arrived on your desk with a third of the pieces pinched, filched, or lost in the mail. Lucky you. You're the gumshoe in charge of putting it all together—under a bare lightbulb, at midnight, with a client looking over one shoulder and the landlord looking over the other.

But you wouldn't trade your work for a year's supply of centerfolds because it reminds you that the gumshoes who succeed in the story detective game are the gumshoes who work with the fewest pieces missing. It's all about what the working stiffs, the ones in suits who punch in at 9 and punch out at 5, call the "details."

You know all about details.

The hero was a good boy, a quiet boy, a polite boy. He chewed with his mouth closed. He sneezed into his elbow. The world never met a hero it didn't like. The gumshoes who stops right there might as well open up the puzzle box and find it empty. You know how that works. More than once you've stared into the cardboard abyss. If every case where you've skipped over the details were a penny, the coin-counting machine at the supermarket would be sending you thank-you cards.

That's why you're such an admirer of Jessica Fletcher. Mrs. F. is the only detective you know with a soft outside and a tough inside, like a Tootsie Roll Pop turned inside out. When she got that feeling in her gut, the one that told her someone was holding back, she turned into the nosy neighbor who never came directly at you. Maybe her gut noticed the muscle car parked in front of the town flirt's house, the one parked there well past midnight.

"Isn't that just like the car I've seen Enrico, your pool boy, drive to church on Sunday?" she might say to the flirt. "I was a bit surprised to see it in front of your house so late at night. Can he do much work on the pool in the dark, especially when your husband's away and not there to hold a flashlight?"

Then, just as the flirt wishes she had two friends named Louie and Big Mike to hustle Mrs. F. back to wherever she came from, Mrs. F. allows that it isn't any of her business and Enrico was probably working in the shed on the filter system and wouldn't the flirt like a cup of tea?

Over tea, the flirt blurts out the whole sordid tale. It's an old story about her philandering husband, and Trixie, her husband's new main squeeze. And about the hotel 20 miles outside of Cabot Cove where they rendez-vous, the website her husband's been ordering lingerie from, Enrico's soft shoulder, and where she hides the door key for him. And the fact that there hasn't been water in the swimming pool for three years.

Maybe it's her training as a novelist, but Mrs. F. was one crafty detective who knew that if she could get someone to tell her a story, they'd spill not only the beans, but the mashed potatoes and gravy, too. Mrs. F. and her little stories. Bad for you if you were in her sights, but good for story detectives if they're about to dig up a hero's past.

The last thing you want when you interview a hero's mother about what kind of woman her son would follow out of a bar and into trouble are dry facts and one-word answers. You want those harmless-sounding stories that got Mrs. Fletcher's gut to dance the Charleston.

You know lots of ways of getting people to talk, many of them legal, and a novelist is a great scam for someone who may otherwise seem too nosy, asking too many questions. You pull a notebook out of your desk and copy eight names off your list of usual and not-so-usual suspects. Eight ought to be a good start. They're eight interesting-looking people who are about to tell you more about the hero than they ever planned to say.

INTERVIEWEES

The day's turning gray as you hail a cab and climb inside, you and your novelist's assistants, *who, what, when, where, why,* and their close personal friend *how*. You'll be making lots of stops today, listening to a lot of stories, and drinking a lot of coffee. Did I mention listening to a lot of stories? Long, boring stories. During which you'll take notes, smile politely, refrain from yawning, and keep people talking until they've told you things they probably haven't told anyone since they were trading blood oaths at summer camp. "How did the hero handle frustration?" "Oh, that's interesting. Where was that?" "Gosh, what happened?" "Who else was there?" "What was the biggest problem he ever had to solve?" "How did that go?" "Who helped him?" "Where did you say that was?"

There are a lot of polite smiles and restroom breaks between now and tomorrow, but by then you'll know enough about the hero to ... well, to write one heck of a story about him.

Take that, Mrs. F.

INTERVIEW WORKSHEET

INTERVIEWEE _____

QUESTION	ANSWER

Copy as many times as necessary.

If Mrs. F. were here now, what do you think she'd say about your efforts? Good job? Nice work? Good luck. She'd probably smile and say, "Well, it certainly sounds as if you've learned a lot about the hero. I'll bet he has a special way of handling frustration, anger, and disappointment, and I'd love to hear all about it. Would you like some tea?"

HERO PROFILE SUMMARY

BEHAVIOR	EXAMPLE (WHAT, WHEN, WHERE, WHO)
Frustration	
Anger	
Disappointment	

BEHAVIOR	EXAMPLE (WHAT, WHEN, WHERE, WHO)
Decision-making	
Relationships	
(Add more categories of your own)	

Now Mrs. F. would be smiling. Come to think of it, maybe a cup of tea isn't a bad way to close the door on today. Of course, even though the door is closed, that doesn't mean it's locked. The people you didn't interview may have tales to tell that prove important. There may come a time when we'll need to visit more people and conduct another interview or three.

But, as Mrs. F. would tell you, that's another story.

EXAMPLE

We need a list of people in Francine's background to interview, which means we need to think about where Francine grew up. There's no right or wrong here, but we have to make a choice. Given that Francine will eventually want to make her mark on society, let's choose a smaller town rather than a city. A town affords Francine the opportunity to grow up in more insulated surroundings, with closer social relationships. If she has big dreams, they would almost surely include leaving her hometown for the big world outside.

Wanting to leave home to get away from many sets of prying eyes and yearning for the opportunity to paint her life on the big canvas of New York, Chicago, or Los Angeles can add conflict to Francine's early years. If it turns out the story is better served with her growing up in a large city, we can always change the back story later.

Starting with the idea that Francine grew up in a small town, let's take our general list of suspects from Chapter 3 and make it more specific to life in small towns. We also need to set the time frame for this story. If Francine is near 60 now, that means she grew up in the 1960s and 1970s. Her hometown, and the people in her life, should reflect that.

INTERVIEWEES

Gloria—mother

Arthur—father

Little Joanie—younger sister

Mrs. Callahan—fourth-grade teacher

Mrs. Zander—next-door neighbor

Aunt Carol—mother's older sister

Carl—paperboy

Doc Maxwell—candy-store owner

Tommy—had a crush on Francine in second grade

Grandma Benson—Gloria's mother

Grandpa Benson—Gloria's father

Carla—Francine's closest friend

Mac—snowplow driver

Nellie—town gossip

The list contains some people from the previous chapter, plus others who just popped up during this activity, such as the town gossip (who made her appearance on the list after the list seemed "done"). The same is true for the snowplow driver; he seemed to come out of nowhere. That's the way this brain-sleuthing often goes, and many times those second-effort entries prove surprisingly valuable. The people who dropped off the list didn't seem as interesting, valuable, or relevant as Francine's life came into focus. The car dealer, who struck a fanciful chord in the last chapter, didn't make the cut. He's gone but not forgotten. If he can provide some undiscovered insight into Francine, or if he may make an interesting character in her story, he's still there waiting for us in our notes.

We need to whittle the list down to eight names, at least to start. If we can't get all the information we need from the initial eight, we can always return to the list and pull in more interviewees.

Let's start with Francine's mother, a rather obvious choice, and then her grandpa. Grandfathers and granddaughters have a special bond. Then let's add Nellie, the town gossip. Chances are, if there's a colorful story in Francine's past, true or not, Nellie knows about it. Tommy, her first crush, and her Aunt Carol seem worth pursuing—especially Carol. Sisters often have strong opinions of how their nieces and nephews ought to be raised, and those views may lead to some interesting conflict and storytelling. Doc, the candy-store owner, earns a spot on the list just because he has an interesting profession. In a small town, he gets to see how kids behave when their parents are watching and when they're not. Finally, let's include Mac, the snowplow driver. There's something interesting about kids and snow, plus his name popped up unexpectedly, so maybe he has something important to tell us.

Note that the people who made the list have at least one quality in common (perhaps inadvertently)—conflict. They're all people who are in a position to see conflicts in Francine's early years, either directly, as when Carol and Francine's mother disagree on child rearing, or indirectly, as when Doc observes how Francine and her mother interact. Conflict is the mother's milk of storytelling, and a good story detective is always on the lookout for conflict, wherever it's hiding.

Now that we have eight people to interview, let's talk to them, keeping in mind the topics we need to elaborate on—the challenges heroes face as they travel through a story. Although it may seem strange to interview a make-believe character, this technique works remarkably well. Pretending to be someone else allows you to say, or write, thoughts the real you may not feel comfortable expressing. Plus, as a screenwriter, you have to pretend to be the characters in your screenplay to write their dialogue and behaviors. These interviews are excellent practice for the role playing you'll do when you tackle your script.

Here are three examples culled from the eight interviewees on our list.

INTERVIEW WORKSHEET

INTERVIEWEE _____ *Gloria (mother)* _____

QUESTION	ANSWER
What was Francine like growing up?	A handful. A real handful. I used to think how lucky the other mothers were that their kids would stand quietly at their sides while they were shopping or talking. Francine, she would go on and on, babbling. Couldn't stand still for a minute.
So she was hard to control?	Control? There was none of that. Francine went her own way.
Could you give me an example of that?	Just one? Well, let me see.... One time, Francine must have been about 8, my mother and father were coming over for Sunday dinner and Francine was playing in the living room with some blocks or toys or something. I tell her, "Francine, it's time to get cleaned up for dinner." That girl doesn't move. So I tell her again. Finally, I just walk in there and start putting away those toys, and do you know what? That girl bit me. Can you imagine that? Drew blood and everything. Then, while I'm patching myself up, she's taking out her toys and playing again.
Did she get along well with people?	You don't know very much about her, do you? She got along _too_ well with people. I mean, there were times when I was downright ashamed to be seen with that girl. For myself, you understand. Ever since she was that high [Gloria holds her hand about 2 feet off the ground], she was always grabbing and hugging people.
So she was affectionate?	Hell, no. She'd do that to total strangers. It was embarrassing. The mailman, he'd come up the walk and she'd run out to meet him and throw her arms around him. I think she was kissing boys at school before she knew how to read and write. I know people talked about her behind my back. Do you know how that makes a mother feel?

When did she leave home?	Oh, her father and I talked a lot about that, and we decided it would be the best for all of us if she left as soon as she turned 18. And she did, too, thanks to that Horace fellow. I guess Francine loved him, but it was hard to tell, seeing as she hugged and kissed everybody that way. 'Course, all of this that happened, that's all Horace's fault. Not that I'm surprised. Francine never did have the smarts of the rest of the family.
You mean the bank robberies?	I don't want to talk about that.
When was the last time you spoke to Francine?	About five years ago, right after she and Horace retired and moved to upstate New York. She said she and Horace wanted me to come out and see their new place. It was just me then. Edward, God rest his soul, passed on about six years before. Francine kept telling me about what a nice place it was, quiet and all, and how they had an extra room. I didn't go.
Why not?	Why not? 'Cause they wanted me to move in with them.
Is that what Francine said?	Didn't have to. I know my daughter.

INTERVIEW WORKSHEET

INTERVIEWEE _____ *Carla* _____

QUESTION	ANSWER
How long have you known Francine?	We go back all the way to high school. We're BFFs. Don't look at me like that. I have grandkids. You have grandkids, you have Facebook. You have Facebook, you have BFFs.
What do you think led to the bank robberies?	What do I look like, a shrink? I'm a housewife. I do a little interior design work. What do _you_ think led to it?
I don't know. I'm trying to find out.	She's got a great husband and a great life. I mean, it's nothing spectacular. She's not Marilyn Monroe or anything. And no kids. I think kids would have made a difference. But she wasn't starving. She lives in a nice house. Horace waited on her hand and foot. Go figure.

So this was totally unexpected?	You're a little slow on the uptake, aren't you? Of course it was expected.
I don't understand.	She _wishes_ she was Marilyn Monroe. She had looks, talent, ambition, smarts—and yet she's working in a post office married to some guy who designs buttons. What do you think was going to happen?
You mean she just snapped?	You really do have to find a new line of work. I said she didn't have any kids. How come you're not asking me why?
Okay. Why didn't she have any kids?	Because she didn't want the competition. Look, she didn't get a lot of love when she was growing up. She had to be Miss Proper Young Lady. She finally gets a chance to haul her ass out of town—and since you're not good at filling in the blanks, that would be Horace taking her away—and she wants all the things she didn't get when she was growing up. Mainly, that's love and attention.
I thought you said you weren't a shrink?	I'm not. But I'm not a complete idiot, either. She doesn't have kids so she has the room to be one. I've seen it a thousand times.
Would you say she hates kids?	No, I think she loves them. She once showed a group of kids around the post office. She raved about her job, her co-workers. She didn't have the heart to tell them it was the worst place on Earth to work.
Do you think what she's doing is right?	The bank robberies? I think if she's doing it she has a good reason. You may not think it's a good reason, but how long do you think you would last in the post office? So what's your opinion worth?

INTERVIEW WORKSHEET

INTERVIEWEE _____ *Mac (snowplow driver)* _____

QUESTION	ANSWER
How well did you know Francine?	She lived in this house on the north side. That's the side that got plowed first, on account of the mayor had his sister-in-law living there, and if she couldn't walk down the block to see her friend, Ellen, there'd be hell to pay. So as soon as the snow stopped, why I was out there on the north side, and there was Francine out there playing in the snow like she didn't have a care in the world.
That doesn't sound unusual.	I guess I forgot to mention. She's got to have been 15 or 16. She's making snowmen and snow houses. She's like one of those developer people over in Middleton. Got herself her own snow town there.
Why did you think this was strange?	You mean besides her being a teenager and all? It was the way she did it. Very careful-like. She didn't just grab some snow and shove it together like other kids did. She'd look. And think. And look some more. Almost like she was building real people. I think there was something wrong with her.
Wrong? In what way?	Well, once I was coming by, and she'd built this whole town right there in front of her house. And I stopped and I kind of asked her what she was doing it all for. I didn't mean nothing by it. I was kind of curious, that's all. I mean, maybe I'm just making conversation. She turns to me and she wants me to knock it all down with my plow. Everything. All these homes and snow people. Well, I'm not going to do it. It must have taken her hours, and it wasn't bothering nobody. It's not in anybody's way. I told her it looked beautiful and maybe her mom and pa would like to see it before it melted. Next thing I know she starts crying. Begging me to knock it down.
Did you?	Like I said, it wasn't bothering anybody. Why would she want it knocked down? But she said I should give her the keys to my plow and she'd knock it down.
What did you do?	I didn't want to do it. But she's standing in my way. Right in the middle of the road. She's not going to budge. And I've got to get to the mayor's sister-in-law. What else was I supposed to do?

The details in these stories not only help define the outlines of Francine's character, they also serve as starting points for her behavior in the future. A young girl who could be so demanding of Mac, a public servant, could be expected to be equally demanding of other public servants—say police officers—in the future. Bank robber or no, she may certainly order them around as it suits her purposes and, as Mac said, "She's not going to budge."

The Hero Profile Summary contains information gleaned from interviews (both those in the previous example and others who, for the sake of brevity, aren't included here) with people in Francine's past. Rearranging the information this way makes it easier to see Francine's predilections for handling challenges and resolving issues. People change, of course, and Francine's future behavior may not exactly mirror what she's done in the past. Nevertheless, there's a good chance that traces of the old Francine will surface in a new Francine, the one who's been transformed by her travels through the story.

HERO PROFILE SUMMARY

BEHAVIOR	EXAMPLE (WHAT, WHEN, WHERE, WHO)
Frustration	Very physical and demonstrative when she doesn't get her way. All the rules of decorum seem to vanish. She bit her mother over a simple disagreement. She cried when the snow-plow driver wouldn't accede to her wishes.
Anger	Also very physical. She smashed the snow village she obviously spent hours building. Although Mac couldn't tell us why she did it, Carla indicated Francine's childhood was less than happy. Francine may have created a childhood scene just to destroy it—to make it go away.

BEHAVIOR	EXAMPLE (WHAT, WHEN, WHERE, WHO)
Disappointment	Descriptions of her disappointment over life are mixed. Carla says the signs were there, yet recalled that Francine could tell a story that completely belied her true feelings. It seems as if Francine bottles up disappointment until it reaches the boiling point. Then she explodes.
Decision-making	Francine seems very deliberate. Mac describes her as being very thoughtful when she was designing her snow village and not clumping and piling snow together like other kids often do.
Relationships	By all accounts, Francine has the capability to form deep relationships, as her marriage with Horace seems to indicate. She also uses her femininity to form relationships with men. She hugs and kisses, as her experiences with Doc Maxwell, the candy-store owner, indicated. Her mother and grandfather both agree Francine is outwardly affectionate, and it seems that's a tool she uses to get her way. She also seems to be solitary. She plays alone, in the snow, rather than with friends. She has only one close adult friend. None of the people interviewed mention close childhood friends or relationships.
(Add more categories of your own) Patience	Francine seems to be able to wait things out. She had a very dull job at the post office, but she stuck it out for years. She seemed to be building up toward something in her life, but she waited to make her move. While she has a tendency to lose her temper, as with the snow village, it seems Francine is able to keep things inside her, almost as if she toggles between patience and frustration.

What's notable here, and why this activity is so useful, are the details that emerged from these interviews. Even from the few in this example, Francine is beginning to emerge as a quixotic and conflicted person—just the sort of person who would turn to bank robbery, or something equally extreme, to solve her perceived problem.

Chapter 5

The Case of the Hero's Behind

A good night's sleep makes it a little easier for you to face the awful truth. Life would be a hell of a lot better if you were the love child of Jessica Fletcher and Gil Grissom. You've seen Grissom take a notebook full of conflicting witness reports, shell casings, loose hubcaps, and a three-block-long string of police cars with enough holes in them to make them naturalized Swiss citizens, and reconstruct the events in a shootout leading up to the death of a policeman.

Reconstruct is hardly the word. Grissom knew everything about the fatal, blue-blood-dripping bullet from the trajectory it took right down to whether the shooter preferred paper or plastic.

Okay, maybe the paper or plastic part is a bit of story detective bravado. The point is, there's finally a stack of paper on your desk bigger than the unpaid bills—it's the notes and background info you've collected on the hero. Short of thinking about how good it's going to feel to spend the "remuneration commensurate with results" that stack of paper represents, the only thing on today's calendar is re-creating the hero's past.

You pick up a file folder from the clutter on your desk. Sure, it's not the world's best filing system, but it's *your* filing system—and since the cleaning lady quit, there's no one around to help you lose things under the guise of trying to keep you "organized." You find that marker you know you have, the black one that's been with you longer than any woman, and label the folder.

HERO DOSSIER

You sit back and look at what you've written so far. Everything's spelled correctly. There's attention to detail (you would've inherited that from Grissom). Making it into a story, that's where Mrs. Fletcher's genes must come in. You need a few pages of prose that paint a picture of how the hero got from where he started to where he is now (right when those "certain friends and acquaintances" brought you into the case). You have a feeling you'll be reading and rereading the story of the hero's life over and over, looking for clues as to what he's going to do next.

Time to turn that pile of paper into the hero's this-is-your-life moment. You pull out the hero dossier forms from the bottom drawer of your desk. Forms—another trait inherited from Grissom.

You reach for a pen and start to write. Did you actually begin with the words, "Once upon a time there was a hero who …"? You pause for a moment and wonder why so many men turn out like their mothers.

HERO DOSSIER

HERO'S NAME _____

EARLY YEARS (where born, raised to age 13, give or take)

TEEN YEARS (school, growing up, dating)

ADULT YEARS (jobs, career, plans, life)

PRESENT (last month before case started)

ADDITIONAL INFO (weaknesses, fears, vulnerabilities, strengths)

EXAMPLE

While writing Francine's dossier, a narrative of the high and low points of her life, from birth up to the start of the story, we may find that our interviews didn't give us all the answers. That's fine; they weren't supposed to. What they did give us is a thumbnail sketch of the hero so that, with the dossier, some brain-sleuthing can do the rest of the work. That said, if we get stuck, if parts of Francine's life feel important but aren't in sharp focus, we can interview more people from her past (or pepper a previous interviewee with follow-up questions).

HERO DOSSIER

HERO'S NAME _____ *Francine* _____

EARLY YEARS (where born, raised to age 13, give or take)

Francine was born in a small town outside Boise, Idaho. For 10 years she was an only child, until one day her sister came along. Francine's mother, Gloria, was never the doting type. Gloria was the youngest of eight children and received barely a dollop of love from her own parents. As a result, she looked to Francine for the attention she never received as a child. Joan (or Little Joanie, as she was known in the family), was an inconvenience, and Gloria was glad to leave much of the mothering of her younger child to Francine.

At the same time, Gloria felt guilty for shunning her responsibilities, so her attitude toward Joan alternated between annoyance and guilt. If she punished Joan, she quickly made up for it by spoiling her. Francine was trapped in the middle. She had a difficult time getting attention from her mother, although Joan seemed to have little trouble. All Joan needed to do was act as if she had been wronged. To compete, Francine adopted a more dramatic style of behavior. She was prone to tantrums, physically demonstrating her displeasure in ways that Gloria couldn't miss. Once, when angry at her mother for interrupting her playtime, a playtime that caught Francine deep in thought, Francine bit her mother. What was so dramatic for Gloria was the way Francine did it. Gloria felt it was instinctive, a reflex—almost like an animal going after food. To Francine, however, it was the end product of something she'd been planning for quite a while. She wondered how biting her mother would turn out, whether she'd be able to do it, and what the repercussions would be. The act was somewhere between a reaction and careful planning.

At a young age, Francine demonstrated she had the patience to choose a path and follow it when she felt the time was right. This wouldn't be the last time Francine's feelings expressed themselves so explosively. Nor would it be the last time she acted out with such physical intensity.

As a young child, Francine was flirty. Preadolescent flirting isn't unusual in young girls, but Francine used it to control the world around her. It was not uncommon to see her hug or kiss total strangers, and she was even more affectionate with those she knew. Once, to score some candy from Doc Maxwell—the owner of the town's only candy store—she built a platform of chairs so she could crawl up and kiss him on the cheek. Kissing became a ritual; with it, Francine not only got candy on a regular basis, but also learned quite a bit about controlling male behavior.

The one word everyone applied to Francine was clever. She was a creative, inventive child, whether it came to getting what she wanted or taking care of her younger sister with minimal impact on her own life. Behind the scenes, though, there were signs that Francine would continue to be a handful when she grew up.

TEEN YEARS (school, growing up, dating)

In school, Francine could be a devil or the teacher's pet, depending on how she felt about the teacher. She was a flirt who attracted boys the way the proverbial honey attracts flies, but she didn't go all the way. The boys considered her a tease, and most of the older boys gave up chasing her. There were always some younger ones or older guys who didn't mind hitting their heads into brick walls who would pursue her, and the whole process amused Francine. At this tender age, she seemed hell-bent on never settling down with a man. She saw boys—and men, by extension—as people who needed severe taking care of. Having gone through (and still going through) that process with Joan, Francine simply wasn't interested.

Francine was desirable for reasons that went beyond her flirting. She was one heck of a student. It was that patient streak in her; she could sit down with her books and study so hard the rest of the world slipped away. Francine was far from a genius, but what she lacked in intelligence, she made up for in pure determination. If you were her classmate and had problems with your homework, Francine was the person to see. If you were nice to her, you may get close to her. If she didn't like you, she'd still help you out, but her tone would be frosty enough to chill a beer keg.

Francine met Carla in high school, and they became fast friends when Carla went to bat for her when she was accused of cheating on an American history exam. One of the better students in the class, apparently willing to trade his grade for a party the night before the test, came to class totally unprepared. He copied answers from Francine's paper and, as a result, both of them turned in papers with the same pattern of right and wrong responses. The teacher, never Francine's fan, assumed she was the culprit. The flap resulted in a suspension for Francine. Carla, who was fiercely loyal, stormed into the principal's office and vaguely threatened him with an assault charge if he didn't investigate the situation and reinstate Francine. Within a few hours, Francine was back in school.

ADULT YEARS (jobs, career, plans, life)

Francine met Horace at a supermarket in Boise. She stood in the aisle, fascinated by this somewhat handsome man who was loading his shopping cart with just about every can of creamed corn on the shelf. She was compelled to watch and count the cans, 23 in all, until she had to know what he was doing.

In her own flirty way, she discovered that Horace was an artist, something Francine didn't believe, and that these cans were the raw materials for his next project. Francine demanded proof of Horace's artistic standing. He seemed somewhat taken aback by her skepticism, so he added a package of dried wagon wheel pasta to his cart and said that if she gave him her name and address, he'd come over at 8 and show her his work.

Francine was staying with a friend who dutifully found a reason not to be home that evening. When Horace arrived, he cheerfully announced that she would have the honor of wearing his first-ever pasta dress, which he would make by replacing the buttons on her dress with wagon wheel pasta. Francine tried to discern whether this was some kind of joke, but Horace's enigmatic expression never wavered. She decided to call his bluff and, in her best flirty style, told him he could have anything he wanted. Horace replied rather offhandedly that he wanted Francine to take off her dress so he could get to work.

In that moment, Horace did what no other boy had ever done: he called her bluff. Her first impulse was to refuse, but standing in front of him, with that indescribable look on his face, Francine didn't know what to do. So she took off her dress. For the first time she could recall, Francine felt vulnerable—truly vulnerable. She put her entire trust in Horace, who was still standing there, smiling.

The rest is history. They made love. Horace returned for Francine the following spring, as soon as he graduated from Reed College. Moving to their new home outside New York City, Francine felt happy for the first time she could remember. She was about to embark upon a new life with someone who didn't demand that she give, give, give. Horace landed a job in the fashion industry. The world looked wonderful.

PRESENT (last month before case started)

Francine's life with Horace had its ups and downs. His career in fashion never really caught fire, but he was content to work as a button designer and continued to pursue his passion for art. Horace's art was a bit outside the mainstream. He liked to blow up things—canned goods, to be exact—and then document the results.

With her almost infinite patience, Francine was more than happy to wait for Horace to succeed. She supported him by not hounding him to get a better or a better-paying job. When they needed money, she went to work at a post office mail distribution center, where she keyed in the first three digits of the ZIP codes on letters so they could be routed automatically. It was a mindless job, but it suited Francine quite well. It left her time to think and dream, and when she came home, Horace was always there, ready to meet her emotional and physical needs. To Francine, life was good.

Then, one day, it was less good. It's not that her life changed; it was that <u>she</u> had. The years had slipped silently by, and now she was approaching 60. Horace was still designing buttons. Francine was wondering where her life had gone. She was struck by the realizations that they had no kids and that Horace wasn't a well-known artist. Sooner rather than later, they'd both be gone, and nobody would even know they'd existed.

Francine became morose. The physical flashes of anger that had marked her childhood reappeared as she felt her life becoming increasingly empty. Horace, somewhat set in his ways, didn't know what to do, although he wanted to do <u>something</u>. He suggested they travel, but Francine scoffed at that. She talked more frequently of the good times growing up in Idaho, something that scared Horace a bit because she rarely dwelled on the past.

He thought a visit back home might cheer up Francine, or that such a visit might exorcise whatever demons were still left in Francine's soul. So off they went to visit Joan and her son, Stanley. The visit began with Francine being morose, but it ended happily. Stanley needed to find a relative with a job interesting enough for his class's upcoming career day, and Francine stepped in to save the day.

Francine returned home with a renewed sense of vigor. Horace noticed it, but he wasn't sure where it was coming from, or where it was headed.

ADDITIONAL INFO (weaknesses, fears, vulnerabilities, strengths)

Weaknesses: Not physically strong, prone to flashes of anger, could be headstrong at times, depressed her real feelings, manipulative

Fears: Abandonment, getting old, dying without a legacy, long and lingering illnesses, that someone would discover how vulnerable she was

Vulnerabilities: Loneliness, not as tough as she appears to be

Strengths: Loyalty, intelligence, patience, good looks, creativity, quick read of people

New ideas popped up out of the dossier. Although none of the people interviewed talked about Francine's high school days, that section of the dossier seemed to flow from what they did say about her as a child. A new person entered Francine's life—her nephew, Stanley—who hadn't been mentioned in any of the interviews. That's one of the advantages of writing down the hero's life as a narrative rather than in, say, bullet points. Our creative faculties become absorbed in the storytelling, and suddenly ideas pour out onto the page. The trick is to put down whatever comes into your mind. You can always add to, reject, modify, or ignore details later. But if the ideas never make it onto the page, we'll never know where the hero was, so we'll have that much more difficulty figuring out where he's going.

Chapter 6

The Case of the Too-Personal Problem

Today you're having a story detective nightmare.

Maybe that's because what started as an intense period of deep thought turned into an afternoon nap. Maybe all those hours of listening to stories finally proved you're as sagging and haggard-looking as your new driver's license photo makes you appear. Maybe it's what happens in a business where following heroes' footsteps makes you tired of playing Ginger Rogers to their Fred Astaire.

Maybe it's every detective's nightmare. That the client they're crawling in bed with is waiting to knife them in the back.

After all, Jim Rockford worries his client will stiff him on his $200 a day plus expenses. Barnaby Jones worries his sweet, innocent client is actually running some scam. Adrian Monk worries his client will hug him.

Your nightmare's been nagging at you like one of those itches that's too low to reach over your shoulder and too high to reach coming up from your belt.

When you're on the trail of a hero who wants something desperately, you need to be sure the hero deserves to get it. Otherwise, when you reach the end of your story, those voices in your head will quickly decide the "remuneration commensurate with results" is nothing more than a heartfelt "Who cares?"

The only time you get paid is when the voices think the hero is a four-square guy—or foursquare enough that they want him to win. It's the hero who wants to get his life savings back to rescue the orphanage where he grew up, the hero who wants to cure cancer to save his mother, the hero who boosts cars to buy his sweetie an engagement ring, the hero who wants to keep her brother from marrying the wrong girl, the hero who wants to save the planet ….

The dime-a-dozen hero may now cost a quarter, but you can still trip over one walking down the street or scraping up your dog's poop. Even with everything you've learned, it's still hard to tell which side of the grabbing-the-goodies-for-me fence this hero you're stalking is likely to fall on. Now that you're fully awake, you need to figure it out. You reach into your pocket, pull out the first scrap of paper you can find, and start doodling ideas.

What happens if the hero doesn't solve his problem?

Who else will be affected if the problem isn't fixed?

What wrong will continue un-righted?

What mistake will go uncorrected?

Will some deserving person not get the help they need?

Will innocent people lose an opportunity?

You turn over the sheet of paper and stare at what you now see is a bill, thinking how much easier it would be to read what it's for if it didn't have the big, red PAST DUE stamped all over it. Surely, you think, Rockford, Jones, and Monk must have dozens of unworthy clients hidden in their closets. Well, maybe not Barnaby Jones, but Rockford and Monk for sure. This time you may just take the case, pocket whatever you can get, and figure out some way to avoid winding up in the same bar with Jones so you won't have to look him in the eye. Anyway, it wouldn't hurt to elaborate a bit on the notes you just made.

BIGGER THAN THE HERO

What happens if the hero doesn't solve his problem?

Who else will be affected if the problem isn't resolved?

What wrong will continue un-righted?

What mistake will go uncorrected?

Will some deserving person not get the help they need?

Will innocent people lose an opportunity?

Okay, so maybe the hero's not your type. Maybe, like the guy hustling three-card monte on the corner, he's someone you need to steer clear of. Maybe, for the sake of quieting those voices in your head, there's something you missed—a quiet injustice in the hero's life, perhaps? People near or close to the hero—people you know about and people you don't? Maybe someone the hero doesn't know yet? A casual acquaintance from his past, perhaps. Is there someone out there who—directly or indirectly—needs the hero's help?

A little brain-sleuthing couldn't hurt. Besides, there's still more doodling room on the back of that bill. (You have some big bills.)

You push the idea of those bills and all other distractions out of your mind. Will solving the problem make the hero a better person? Could he go out drinking milk with Barnaby Jones with a clear conscience? Will it give the hero a chance to help other people become better off? Will solving the problem right a wrong or help somebody find something he or she has lost? You don't want to turn all soft here, but to a lot of people, love, honor, pride, and respect count as much as money, fame, and a fancy house by the ocean.

THE HERO'S WORTH IT

WHO	WHAT'S THE PROBLEM?	HOW DOES SOLVING THE HERO'S PROBLEM HELP?	WHY DOES THIS MAKE US ROOT FOR THE HERO?

Time to look at what you've written. Is it specific? Does solving the problem let the hero "help his friend" or "help his friend get a job and save his marriage"? What stands out? What one thing on your list looks like something the hero should be fighting for? There's one line left at the bottom of the bill. Use it to sum it all up.

If the hero solves his problem, he will benefit because _____

_____

_____, *and* _____

_____ *will benefit because* _____

_____.

What's the score? Would soft-spoken, homespun Barnaby Jones see through this hero as a phony? Do you need to pound the sidewalks a bit more, retrace your steps, add some names to your interview list, and see what's really going on behind the hero and what he's after? Or is it time to cut your out-of-pocket losses, eat burgers instead of filet mignon for a while, and wait until those voices call back with a real case?

It's too hard to decide right now. You put your feet up on your desk. This is a decision that deserves an intense period of deep thought.

Like they all do.

E X A M P L E

Francine has a problem. She's closer to the end of her life than the beginning and, without kids, she's starting to imagine a world where there are no traces of her existence. Her solution is to become somebody by robbing banks.

Bonnie and Clyde and Butch Cassidy and the Sundance Kid notwithstanding, the life of a bank robber is overly romanticized in our society. In reality, you rob a bank, and in short order, some obsessive-compulsive law enforcement officers will be on your trail. While the "occupation" comes with a certain amount of notoriety, in the long run, that notoriety probably won't earn you any Facebook friends.

When Francine and Horace are tired of looking over their shoulders while scoring slushy drinks at the convenience store, what's going to keep them from concluding that they've had their fun and bailing out of the story?

Nothing. Francine and Horace can invest their meager bounty in the underworld's equivalent of witness protection and, with some plastic surgery, fake passports, and a pair of one-way plane tickets to somewhere, they can enjoy the rest of their lives in freedom and anonymity. And even if they decide to stay in the game, why should anyone care?

BIGGER THAN THE HERO

What happens if the hero doesn't solve his problem?

What happens if Francine dies without making her mark? Sadly, not much. She goes to her grave like 99.9 percent of the rest of the world.

Who else will be affected if the problem isn't resolved?

Her family, some friends, and perhaps an enemy or two. Maybe one or two equally anonymous people whose lives she's touched.

It's not the mark Francine hoped to make, but she wouldn't be in a position to concern herself with it anymore.

What wrong will continue un-righted?

Philosophers can argue over this one, and how anonymity and the desire to be remembered affect the human condition. As an objective story detective, the answer in Francine's case has to be "there's no wrong that would make for a good story."

What mistake will go uncorrected?

Plenty of mistakes will go uncorrected—all in Francine's life. She should have gone to college. She shouldn't have married Horace. She ought to have answered that ad in the paper for dancers at the Boom-Boom Club. Not much anybody can do about any of these things.

Will some deserving person not get the help they need?

This idea of Francine's was all hers. Maybe Horace got a kick out of being in the public eye, or maybe he went along with Francine out of love or a sense of duty. But there hardly seems anything about Horace that makes him any more or less deserving than anybody else.

Will innocent people lose an opportunity?

No, just some money, one way or another. After all, FDIC insurance covers all bank depositors.

At this point, at least from a story detective's point of view, the case of Francine and Horace is a 24-karat nonstarter.

It's hard to see why, if Francine's story were made into a film, the average person would root for her or believe she deserves to make her mark. She's just another person living a disappointing life who's trying to improve it. To take on her case and get the audience on her side, we need to see how Francine's desire might affect the people around her who deserve help.

That's a good rule of thumb, too. When looking for the bigger effect of the hero's problem, keep focused on people who will be affected, not institutions. The hero may want to help the orphanage where he grew up, but what's the personal connection? One of the kids in the orphanage who's having a rough time? The head of the orphanage with whom the hero had a previous relationship? Good story detectives follow people, not things.

Let's imagine who in Francine's world might be affected, who Francine might knowingly or unknowingly be able to help. These could be people we've already interviewed or people we're inspired to make up on the spot. As part of the brain-sleuthing process, we only need to follow the flow of our ideas and imagination.

THE HERO'S WORTH IT

WHO	WHAT'S THE PROBLEM?	HOW DOES SOLVING THE HERO'S PROBLEM HELP?	WHY DOES THIS MAKE US ROOT FOR THE HERO?
Horace	Horace is an "unknown," too.	Francine's fame may translate into money for Horace.	She's doing it for her husband.
Parents	Her parents don't feel they did a good job raising Francine.	Francine's parents can point to her fame and accomplishment.	We all want our parents to be proud of us.
Horace	Francine is miserable in her life.	Horace has done all he can to console Francine to no avail, but robbing banks may make her happy.	Francine knows this will make her husband happier, too.
Francine's snobbish relatives	Relatives are embarrassed that underachieving Francine is part of the family.	Relatives can brag that she's part of the family.	Francine has a strong sense of family responsibility.
Nephew	Nephew is picked on at school because he comes from an "underachieving" family.	Nephew can be proud of someone in his family.	Francine wants to help her nephew, a kid who doesn't deserve to be picked on, when no one else can or will.
Carla	Carla could use more visibility in her life.	A famous Francine would help Carla achieve her goal.	Francine wants to help Carla more than she wants to help herself.

Most of the entries are ho-hum. They can be reduced to "if Francine succeeds and makes her mark, then somebody else gets to feel good, too." The problem is, these somebody elses aren't all that deserving, either. From what we've learned about Francine's mother, for example, she wasn't the best mom in the world, and it's not evident that her feeling good because Francine succeeds is enough of a reason for us to root for Francine.

Two entries, though, are worth considering because they're plausible but not commonplace. The idea that her nephew might not get picked on in school because he's associated with someone famous is worth exploring. The nephew entry is more specific than the "relatives" entry, although the former was inspired by the latter. Specific is good. Stories are helped along by specific details.

Carla's entry is also interesting. Although we didn't get a sense of her occupation in her background interview, she might hold a job where an affiliation with a notorious person could help. Imagine Carla's a newspaper reporter at the end of her career, someone who needs one more boost—just one more scoop—before retiring. Or visualize Carla working for a boss who's both star-struck and in the throes of choosing employees to lay off. Being the close personal friend of a daring bank robber might be just what Carla needs to hold on to her job for a few more years.

How do you choose? Easy. Make your best guess. There's no magic formula. Just make a choice.

If the hero solves her problem, she will benefit because _she will get to live out her dream to make her mark_ , and _her nephew_ will benefit because _he'll be the kid at school others look up to instead of the kid everybody picks on_ .

Kids can be cruel, picking on each other in uncalled-for ways for reasons adults can't fathom. The notion that other kids pick on Francine's nephew, Stanley, because he comes from a dull family is unusual, but it's not all that far-fetched. Francine might need some excitement in her life, but with Stanley's problem, she's doubly motivated to do something about it. Stanley's plight gives Francine a motive that extends beyond herself. She wants to help an innocent kid who doesn't deserve to be tormented just because he was unfortunate enough to be born into Francine's family. Let's see where this choice takes us.

Chapter 7

The Case of the Beached Client

The "certain friends and acquaintances" are back. They want to know what kind of progress you've made. Except every time they bring up the word *progress,* they keep putting the words *lack of* ahead of it.

You try explaining, respectfully, that although they have presented you with a very interesting case and, respectfully, the hero seems like a decent and deserving sort, you need to know one more thing about him before you actually commit to stalking him.

Respectfully.

The "certain friends and acquaintances" have no problem with this, except for the part wherein they believe they've already hired you and that you're their guy. Fortunately, they've stopped using the words *lack of.* Unfortunately, they are now starting sentences with "Don't take this as a threat, but …." As a story detective, you do what story detectives do best when faced with unpleasant situations.

You tap dance.

"Imagine," you begin, "the sun rises over a deserted tropical island." The silence in your head is pregnant with anticipation, so you press on.

> An infinite stretch of pure, white sand is interrupted by two lone figures. One, wearing a Speedo bathing suit, sits in a beach chair. The other, wearing a rumpled trench coat, badly scuffed shoes, and a head of hair that looks like he slept in it, stands over him.
>
> The first guy is the hero of a story. He's been missing for weeks. The best story detectives in the world have been looking for him.
>
> A real Houdini, this guy.
>
> Everybody pooled their resources and brought in Lieutenant Columbo. If there's anyone who can unravel a mystery, it's Columbo. Besides, his annoying habit of pestering everyone he meets with questions makes him the unanimous choice to send out of town.
>
> Somehow—and nobody's itching to hear an explanation— Columbo found this deserted tropical island, where he came upon the hero sitting back with an umbrella-laced cocktail in his hand, puffing on a big cigar, feet up, watching the surf. He's the most content hero the world has ever seen.
>
> "You've got to come back with me, sir," Columbo says to the hero.
>
> "Nope," the hero says, wafting a puff of smoke in Columbo's face. "Like it here."
>
> "You know what I think?" Columbo says, "I think there are friends, associates, wives, children, relatives, enemies—an entire world out there—interested in what happened to you. I don't want to tell you how to act, sir, but I think it's a little bit selfish for you to sit here ignoring them."
>
> "Don't care," the hero says, as a smoke ring floats by Columbo's ear. "No car chases, no money problems, no broken romances, no spies with guns, no world coming to an end …." His voice trails off, lost in the sound of the crashing surf.

For 20 minutes, Columbo grills the cringing hero on his reasons for staying. "I guess there's nothing more I can say," Columbo finally says.

"Goodbye would be nice."

Columbo takes a few steps away from the water's edge. "Just one more question," he says, as the hero considers drowning himself in his drink. "Would you have an extra chair and maybe a bathing suit? Something a little larger than that?"

You've just explained a story detective's second-greatest nightmare to the "certain friends and acquaintances." You find the hero way over there, but his story is way back here. What are you going to do?

The voices, the "certain friends and acquaintances," have no idea. And neither do you. "Chances are, not much," you say. "I only deal with heroes who are so bound up in the story that the thought of heading off to a tropical island, or even a stretch of pipe in the New York City sewer system, is just not in the cards."

You want to tell those "certain friends and acquaintances" that when the going gets rough for the hero—and it will—he can easily split, leaving you with a sheaf of out-of-pocket expenses. But you'd rather they not know these innermost details of your business.

At the same time, you don't want to wind up with some very dissatisfied voices in your head. All of which means you must ask yourself an important question—does the hero have a reason to stay in the story?

You take out your notes from yesterday, the one with the hero's bigger problem. There's one more thing to add. Who are all the people involved? How might they be affected if the hero joins Columbo and his new best friend?

HERO CAN'T WALK OUT

HERO'S BIGGER PROBLEM _____

WHO DOES THE PROBLEM AFFECT?	WHAT WOULD HAPPEN IF HERO WALKED OUT?	WHY WON'T HE DO THAT?

It's gotten awfully quiet in your office. Those "certain friends and acquaintances" who were badgering you in your head are gone. You can look over your notes one more time. Does the hero have a problem bigger than himself? Can he stick with solving it, no matter how ugly the solution, without crawling out of bed one morning and asking whether you spell Bora Bora with a hyphen?

If so, there's a chance those voices will leave you alone for a while—and it's a good thing, too.

It looks like you've got yourself a case.

EXAMPLE

As in the last chapter, the hero's relationship with people is what will keep the hero in the story. The hero isn't in the game all by himself. Whatever he wants, whatever he's looking for, and however he's going to change, the results are going to affect somebody else, and it's somebody the hero doesn't want to let down.

Let's work with the people in Francine's life, as we did in the previous chapter. It's not actually important what might or might not happen if the hero walks out of the story. What's important is what the hero *thinks* will happen. Being a good story detective means being able to think like the characters you're tracking down.

HERO CAN'T WALK OUT

HERO'S BIGGER PROBLEM _____Stanley will get picked on and worse_____

WHO DOES THE PROBLEM AFFECT?	WHAT WOULD HAPPEN IF HERO WALKED OUT?	WHY WON'T HE DO THAT?
Stanley	He'll continue to get picked on, and worse.	Francine's nephew's pain is as great, or greater, than her own.
Horace	He'll feel responsible for helping Stanley.	He's never going to feel for Stanley like Francine does.
Her sister Joan	Things won't change for Stanley.	Francine feels she owes it to Stanley because she didn't protect her sister from their mother's poor parenting skills.
Carla	Francine will lose Carla's approval.	Even more than Horace, Carla's support and admiration kept Francine going through rough times.

As often happens in brain-sleuthing, we've discovered more bits and pieces about Francine's life. She doesn't think Horace can do the job of protecting Stanley as well as she can. This sounds as if there might be another area of conflict between Francine and Horace. Good. Conflict can bubble to the surface at the most unexpected and inconvenient times, enriching and enlivening a story. Francine feels guilty for not standing up for her sister when they were kids. What else might she feel guilty about? Carla has been there for Francine through rough times (what were they?), providing the approval Francine hasn't found elsewhere.

The more we know about Francine, the more we know about how she will behave later in the story. We may not know what to do with the information now, but finding it before we need it never hurts.

Part 2

The Caper

Chapter 8

The Case of the Not-So-Lost Baggage

It seems it's time to get out in the field and do the kind of work that got you into the story detective business in the first place—following clues, seeing places that don't look like the four walls of your office, and matching wits with some first-class slime-ball villains.

Let the caper begin.

Not that it's been a while, but … it's been a while, so you have to give some thought to your first move. Maybe sharpening the pencils you'll need for taking notes? Cleaning out the fridge at home? Straightening the pictures on the walls, at least the pictures the sticky tape is still holding up?

Or maybe driving to Neptune, California, to ask for advice from one very disarming detective by the name of Veronica Mars.

Sure, Veronica's only 18, and you'll probably find her serving coffee at The Hut, but the detective business is in her genes. Her old man was one heck of a sheriff before the little incident that forced him into private investigations. She knows her detective work, and she also knows how to sling the lingo, like describing a huge rock of an engagement ring as "a diamond Volkswagen parked on your finger." In a different time, she might have made a swell business partner, a doll who could have been one of the boys.

First thing Veronica would tell you to do is check the hero's baggage. Mars isn't looking for an afternoon of breaking and entering, and she couldn't care less where the hero stands on boxers, briefs, or over-the-calf socks. She's talking about the other baggage heroes carry around. Bank accounts. Friends. Enemies. What they own. What they owe. Who they trust. What they believe. Where they hang out. What they avoid.

She'd rifle her way through a hero's life's baggage, the way she did while tracking down a missing bride-to-be. What got Mars's attention wasn't the bachelorette party the night before, but the removal of an ex-boyfriend's name formerly tattooed on the bride-to-be's cheek (think below the belt), the emergence of a stranger in her life (known only by his bright orange bowling shirt), and a fax from a guy named Nick. How's the missing bride-to-be changing? What baggage is she packing and unpacking? That's what Mars looked for.

Given that you're chasing a hero through a story, you'd better pack your latex gloves because you'll be going through a lot of the hero's baggage yourself.

Whether you know it or not, those "certain friends and acquaintances" are just as interested in the way the story changed their old pal as they are in whether he was popping wheelies on a stolen Harley while drawing a bead on a pair of thugs who were making off with his new main squeeze. Scratch that—they're *more* interested. This new hero is the one they'll be living with in the future, long after that Harley is collecting dust in a *New York Times* movie review.

Right now, you need to think like the old hero, the way he'd start reaching out to friends and dredging up old habits when the story begins closing in on him. The pressure might be gentle at first, but before long, the squeezing will force the confidence out of him like he's a tube of toothpaste underneath a giant thumb.

That's when the hero will begin rummaging through his baggage and dredging up whatever he's got to work with. Bank accounts. Stocks and bonds. Friends. Relatives. Old flames. New flames. Even a few dying embers. Sooner or later, somebody in the hero's circle is going to get that late-night knock on the door and you want to be the second person to know about it.

Who's in the group of people the hero relies on, or might rely on? The hero's family and friends? Perhaps, but there are always footnotes in a hero's life. Every hero knows a guy who knows a guy who knows a guy. The bottled-water delivery driver who has the 411 on every family in the neighborhood. The hero's kid's teacher can make an important introduction. The perky brunette who works behind the supermarket register or the pimply-faced teenager who hustles pedestrians for dollars with his clipboard and a charity ID badge. There are fellow students, business associates, or the homeless guy on the corner.

You list them all out.

Everyone from a person with a vested interest in seeing the hero succeed to someone who would be there out of the goodness of his or her heart.

HERO'S FRIENDS AND ALLIES BAGGAGE

WHO	RELATIONSHIP	HOW MIGHT HELP	REASONS FOR HELPING

WHO	RELATIONSHIP	HOW MIGHT HELP	REASONS FOR HELPING

If you're lucky, the hero has a lot of personal baggage and may be able to handle what's lurking in his future. But that also means you can't interview everybody the hero's ever exchanged handshakes, phone numbers, or good mornings with. So circle your top candidates (at least three, but five would be better), the ones who look like friends or allies who will answer the call if the hero needs them. Like the hero, you need to know how they'll respond when they find themselves in situations they don't want to find themselves in.

How do these friends and allies handle frustration? Relationships? Living outside their comfort zones? Are they supportive, or would they stop and criticize his choice of window treatments if the hero's house were burning down? Before rubbing elbows with villains and slime balls, you need to pull off another round of interviews, just like you did for the hero.

FRIEND/ALLY INTERVIEW WORKSHEET

FRIEND/ALLY _____

INTERVIEWEE _____

RELATIONSHIP TO FRIEND/ALLY _____

QUESTION	ANSWER

Copy as many times as necessary.

While the details are fresh, make up some short dossiers. Copy the worksheet as many times as necessary.

FRIEND/ALLY DOSSIER WORKSHEET

FRIEND/ALLY'S NAME _____

EARLY YEARS (where born, raised to age 13, give or take)

TEEN YEARS (school, growing up, dating)

ADULT YEARS (jobs, career, plans, life)

PRESENT (last month before case started)

ADDITIONAL INFO (weaknesses, fears, vulnerabilities, strengths)

As sure as Mars will ask her old man for help, there's going to come a time in the life of the hero when he's going to have to go it alone. That's when he'll rely on what he's got inside him. Skills. Hobbies. Experiences. Knowledge. Ordinary and not so ordinary possessions, like that stamp collection that can be turned into no-questions-asked cash when the government freezes his bank accounts.

Maybe the hero has access to people or things because of where he works. A hero in need of a car can bust a window and hot-wire a ride if he knows how. Or he can score a job as a valet and wait for people to give him their keys voluntarily.

You never know.

Maybe the hero's traveling light. Maybe he's got a moving van trailing behind him on a short leash. At least you'll be able to keep those "certain friends and acquaintances" abreast of the hero's changes as he loads and unloads his baggage.

HERO'S NONFRIENDS BAGGAGE

FINANCIAL ASSETS	SKILLS/TALENTS	EXPERIENCE	ATTITUDES/BELIEFS

FAVORITE PLACES	HABITS/ACTIVITIES	OTHER	

The least you can do is order a cup of joe from Veronica. Make it a double half-caff skinny latte with two pumps of vanilla, and leave a generous tip.

E X A M P L E

Let's start identifying your hero's baggage by making a quick list of the people in Francine's life who may help her make her mark and help her nephew at the same time. These may be people we've met before or people who just come to mind during the brain-sleuthing process.

HERO'S FRIENDS AND ALLIES BAGGAGE

WHO	RELATIONSHIP	HOW MIGHT HELP	REASONS FOR HELPING
Horace	husband	by doing anything Francine needs him to do	he's deeply in love with her
Stanley	nephew	as a kid he may not have a clear picture of right versus wrong so might help Francine if she needs some questionable things done	he's tired of being picked on he needs someone to look up to
Carla	BFF	tough, convincing and resourceful can be counted on in a pinch	there's a bond there that spans the years desires a taste of fame and excitement

WHO	RELATIONSHIP	HOW MIGHT HELP	REASONS FOR HELPING
Gloria	mother	despite everything, Francine's mother could be there to bail her out of trouble	mothers have been known to lie, cheat, even steal to protect their kids once a mother, always a mother
Alan	investment counselor	can find ways to dig up money, and perhaps other resources, if Francine needs them	has a crush on Francine
Chief Ryan	police chief in town where Francine lives	might be nice to have a lawman on her side	they're good friends

To start, let's narrow down the list to three people. Two of them are givens: Horace and Stanley both need to be on the list. They feel like major characters in the story. So we need to pick one more. Chief Ryan seems the least interesting because his reason for helping is the lamest of everyone on the list. Alan, the investment counselor, is one of those off-the-wall choices; he's not the kind of person one imagines getting mixed up with bank robbers, and the notion that he has a crush on Francine lends itself to some potential fun in their interactions.

Carla might be a better choice. Alan's help is specialized, while Carla's is general. If she's resourceful, Carla may find people like Alan (and Chief Ryan) if and when Francine needs them.

As examples, here are short dossiers, inspired by interviews, for Horace and Stanley.

FRIEND/ALLY DOSSIER WORKSHEET

FRIEND/ALLY'S NAME _____ _Horace_ _____

EARLY YEARS (where born, raised to age 13, give or take)

Horace was born in San Diego, California. From a very early age, he knew he didn't belong there. Everybody described him as a sweet, happy kid with a great sense of humor.

His way out of any bad situation was to clown around, make jokes, and get people laughing.

Once, in elementary school, the school bully went after Horace for his lunch money. Alone in the bathroom and surrounded by the bully and his cohorts, Horace did a dead-on imitation of the bully, from the way he sprayed saliva when he spoke to the way he kept pushing his shirt over his ample waistline and back into his pants. This so infuriated the bully that he beat up his laughing cohorts instead, and he never picked on Horace again.

But San Diego is a Navy town. Horace's father was a serious Navy captain, and his parents' social circle was made up of serious Navy officers. Horace found his environment far too serious for him.

TEEN YEARS (school, growing up, dating)

Throughout high school, Horace had one thought, and that was to get out of San Diego and go someplace fun (although he had no idea where that would be). He was an unremarkable student, but he was quite disciplined. He turned his work in on time, and it was always done well. He enjoyed the sciences because those classes allowed him to exercise his anti-establishment creativity. In chemistry, he routinely submitted lab reports containing pages of meaningless numbers (often baseball scores) because he knew his teacher didn't read the reports in detail. Those reports became legendary among his friends. Years later, after Horace graduated, the reports became public, and his chemistry teacher took early retirement.

Nevertheless, Horace was fascinated by chemistry, chemicals, and, especially, things that went boom. He used to whip up batches of a mild but unstable chemical mixture that he'd paint onto sheets of paper. He'd set the papers on his windowsill and watch flies land on them, only to disappear in dramatic explosions highlighted by puffs of purple smoke.

Throughout high school, Horace dated Tina. Like everything else in Horace's life, she was sturdy and unremarkable. It's unclear whether Horace ever got past second base with her. Tina liked Horace because he wasn't as stuffy as other Navy brats and because he made her little pictures by pasting dried pasta on construction paper.

Horace's dream of leaving San Diego came true when he was accepted into Reed College in Oregon, where he studied art. His mother was proud of him. His father feared Horace might be gay.

ADULT YEARS (jobs, career, plans, life)

At Reed, Horace learned he had a knack for saying the right thing at the right time. It came in handy because what started with flies on his windowsill progressed to an all-out hobby.

Horace liked to blow up things. Not big things, like buildings, but small things, like canned food. Once, he blew up a can of green peas by heating it until it exploded and then he painstakingly measured where every last pea landed. He spent three months re-creating the pattern of splayed peas and shrapnel from the can as a project for one of his art classes. It took a fair amount of explaining to convince the police he was nothing more than a harmless college student pursuing his art.

Horace met Francine when he visited a college friend who lived in Boise. She thought he was cute and strange when they bumped into each other in a supermarket, where Horace was buying about two dozen cans of creamed corn. She didn't believe he was an artist, but she wanted to. Horace bought a package of dried wagon wheel pasta along with all the creamed corn. That night, he came over to her friend's house and convinced her she should wear the first-ever pasta dress, which he created by replacing the buttons on her rather plain dress with the pasta. To do this, Horace insisted, Francine would have to take off her dress. She did. They had sex. They were soul mates after that.

As soon as Horace graduated, he went to Idaho and married Francine, and the two moved to suburban New York City so Horace could take a job in the fashion industry.

PRESENT (last month before case started)

The fashion industry might be glamorous, but not uniformly. Francine dreamed of glittering dresses, endless rounds of parties, celebrities, and the like, but Horace preferred the quiet life, much as he was used to growing up (only without the rigid Navy influence).

Horace worked as a button designer. It wasn't a taxing job, nor were there many opportunities for creativity. In his later years, it was pretty much a question of whether to put two, three, or four holes in a button (or no holes at all and just a small wire loop instead) so it could be sewn onto a garment. That left him time to work on his art, which still consisted of blowing up things and making collages, photographs, or reproductions of the results. Francine supported his artistic bent, both emotionally and financially, the latter with her job at the post office. Horace was incredibly happy, although he sensed Francine was not. He had no idea what to do about it because Francine rarely complained.

ADDITIONAL INFO (weaknesses, fears, vulnerabilities, strengths)

Weaknesses: Francine, explosions

Fears: His old chemistry teacher would come after him, Francine might die before he did, his father

Vulnerabilities: Francine, easily bullied

Strengths: Charming, easy to like, good talker

FRIEND/ALLY DOSSIER WORKSHEET

FRIEND/ALLY'S NAME _____ *Stanley* _____

EARLY YEARS (where born, raised to age 13, give or take)

Stanley is the youngest child of Francine's much younger (by 10 years) sister, Joan (a.k.a. Little Joanie). Joan married late and had kids even later, and that's how, in retirement, Francine ends up with an 8-year-old nephew. Stanley was a normal kid, or as normal as he could be given the family he came from. Joan was an afterthought—a surprise—and she was frequently ignored by her parents. A longing for attention carried over into her adult years, and the result was that Joanie wanted all the attention in the family, attention that should have gone to Stanley.

Not knowing the difference, Stanley was fine with being independent. At 8, he had his own front-door key. If his mother wasn't home when he arrived from school, he was perfectly capable of making himself a peanut butter and jelly sandwich, playing in his room, and doing his homework. Or he often walked down the street to his friend's house, where he would make a peanut butter and jelly sandwich, play in his friend's room, and do his homework.

Stanley was quite outspoken because he learned early that if he wanted something, he would have to ask for it, usually without his mother's help. He was confident in every way ... until his confidence was shattered at school. The teacher arranged for a career day, where parents would talk to the class about what exciting jobs they had. Stanley's father ran off when Stanley was 3, and Joan was hardly in a position to enthrall young minds with her exciting career as a waitress. She hated waitressing, an opinion she shared with everyone, including her customers. In between waitressing jobs, she worked as a maid—another job she hated. There was no way Stanley wanted his mother anywhere near his classmates or his teacher.

Two weeks before the career day, students had to print their parents' names and jobs on the white board in the back of the classroom. The slot next to Stanley's name was conspicuously blank. The teacher, who wasn't insensitive to Stanley's plight, suggested he invite a relative instead of Joan. The only relative he could think of was Aunt Francine, who sat in front of a machine all day, and Uncle Horace, who ... well, nobody really went into detail about Horace to Stanley. He was just Uncle Horace.

ADDITIONAL INFO (weaknesses, fears, vulnerabilities, strengths)

Weaknesses: He's 8 years old, impressionable, insecure

Fears: Afraid he'll wind up alone

Vulnerabilities: Threats of abandonment, being ostracized

Strengths: Self-sufficiency, energetic, smart, curious

Here's an example of some baggage that extends beyond Francine's friends.

HERO'S NONFRIENDS BAGGAGE

FINANCIAL ASSETS	SKILLS/TALENTS	EXPERIENCE	ATTITUDES/BELIEFS
nearly paid-off mortgage government pension	creative Horace good at blowing up things		optimistic patient loyal

FAVORITE PLACES	HABITS/ACTIVITIES	OTHER	
	flirty	inventory of canned goods	

The idea that Francine has an inventory of canned foods was inspired by Horace's art work. It's an unusual enough possession that it might give Francine an edge later on. That makes it worth adding to the list, even if its importance isn't clear right now. Her nearly paid-off mortgage falls in the same category. Most people are far from owning their own homes free and clear. Francine is not. That could be another edge for her. Adding it to the list doesn't hurt.

Note that, as often happens in brain-sleuthing, not every category in every worksheet deserves an entry. Here, for example, Francine has no favorite places. That's fine. The category headings are there to get your ideas flowing. If a category doesn't fit a particular character, so be it. If you can think of other categories that help you out, add them to the worksheet and use them as well.

This completes Francine's dossier—for now. We know quite a bit about who she is, why she's that way, and what resources she's going to have to work with. That's good news … and bad. It's good because as we track her through the story, we'll be called upon to make all manner of decisions, from the names of people she meets to the actions she takes in unfamiliar situations. With this dossier in place, we have some context for making choices.

The bad news is that having all this written down in front of us is deceptive. What we have is the product of our brain-sleuthing, of our wringing or willing the hero into being from our imagination. Having done that work, there's the danger of believing that what we created is impeccable and immutable. Writing is a process of discovery. En route to discovering what our story is, we're going to bump our way through potholes and pitfalls. When that happens, we need to back up or toss aside anything that's not working (or stopped working) for us.

Chapter 9

The Case of the Day-to-Day Case

You've done your homework. You have a pretty good picture of the hero. Maybe it's the kind of picture you could have wormed out of the hero's bartender in 15 minutes with a C-note, but more than likely, the bartender gathered the sordid details from one of the hero's self-pitying diatribes, fueled by several shots of liquor he downed right before last call.

Whatever you know about the hero, there's one thing you can be sure of, one thing nobody's said out loud. He started off the story convinced he had everything under control. Heroes always think they're in charge. It doesn't matter of what. A romance. A business deal. An impossible crime. Heroes will go to great lengths to keep on believing they're the boss, no matter what the real world's telling them.

That C-note you were willing to fork over to the barkeep? You can bet it all that the hero's problem isn't foremost in his mind. Then, let your winnings ride and bet things don't stay that way. If they did, those voices in your head wouldn't be keeping you up at night, interjecting themselves into your thoughts, and disrupting your quality bathroom time. Something must have happened to rock the hero's world, and that doesn't mean he scored a pair of tickets to a Rolling Stones revival tour.

Listen carefully, and you'll discover that those voices in your head dearly want to know what that something was. What was the hero doing, and what happened next? After all that time spent making lists of subjects, interviewing them, and making more lists, it's finally time to dig up the real dirt. Just don't go digging alone.

Don your best Columbo trench coat—although if you know Columbo, you know "best Columbo trench coat" is an oxymoron—and take the lieutenant along with you.

Columbo often arrives on the scene late, usually after parking the lumpy pile of sheet metal he calls a car somewhere where it won't lower property values. By the time Columbo starts his investigation he seems thoroughly confused about what happened, why it happened, and what he's doing there. That's when Columbo does what he does best.

He asks questions.

"Excuse me," he'll say. "Is that the victim?" Given that Columbo is pointing to a fully zipped body bag, you find yourself in that group of people who wonder just how effectively your tax dollars are being spent on his salary.

Columbo also never met a question that didn't have an answer and an answer that didn't upset him. "I'm having trouble with her story." "That's a thought, sir." "You see my problem?" "There's always room for doubt." "That's what we all thought originally. Including myself. But no …."

Pay attention, and you'll see Columbo is not only annoying, but also annoyingly clever. He's not afraid to ask the obvious question, the ordinary question, the silly question. And he'll keep asking questions until the answers add up. Starting now, you're not going to take yes, or no, for an answer. When you're out in the field, silly, obvious, out-of-whack questions and suspicious answers are as much a part of your daily routine as coffee breaks and pit stops.

First, do some brain-sleuthing. You know the hero's problem, and you know he was avoiding it. So what was he doing? How would you characterize the hero's day-to-day life? Dull? Exciting? Depressing? Energizing? What was his general attitude? Angry? Happy? Boring? Carefree? What activities did he get involved in, and what activities summed up his day-to-day life?

Follow Columbo's lead. Run those questions through your brain, roll them around, and see what you come up with. Continue sleuthing with the people, places, and things involved in the hero's day-to-day life. Who did he spend his time with? Where did he spend his time? What events took place as part of his daily routine?

Make a list of what the hero might do, day to day. Then narrow down your list to your best choices.

DAY-TO-DAY ACTIVITIES

Interview people who are part of the routine or who watch it every day, people with firsthand information. Ask your best questions first. Then remember that Columbo rarely leaves the scene without turning back, or looking over his shoulder, and saying, "Excuse me. Just one more question …."

Everyone you interview in this case has three things ahead of them in their lives: death, taxes, and a Columbo question. Ask it on your way out the door.

DAY-TO-DAY ACTIVITIES WORKSHEET

WHO	WHERE	WHAT	EVENTS OF INTEREST	QUOTES FROM WITNESSES

Something entered the hero's life unexpectedly, like a phone call from an old flame the day after you announce your engagement. Nothing that, by itself, put the hero missing in action. More like an opportunity—an opportunity to prove to the world that the problem didn't exist. It's that kind of a I-don't-have-to-call-that-old-flame-back-because-I've-moved-on bravado you tell everyone while simultaneously hitting her speed dial number on your phone.

On that list is something the hero was doing when his problem interjected itself. What was it? How did the problem show up?

The hero was _____ *when*

_____.

Columbo was not one for sitting in his office imagining the world outside. It's doubtful he even knew what his office looked like. He probably needed a map to find it. You've been looking at the inside of your office way too long. You grab your trench coat and make a mental note to stop at that smoke shop on the west side and see if they have Columbo's brand of cigar (old, stubbed down to half its size, and hardly ever lit). It'll give you something to chew on while you take notes at the scene of the action—who, what, where, what was around, and anything else that would catch Columbo's eye.

FIELD REPORT WORKSHEET

PEOPLE	PLACES	EVENTS WORTH NOTING

Knowing what happened is half the story. Knowing where it happened is the second half. Columbo would want to know even more. You know who was there. You may even have some quotes from them. Interview at least the three who can tell you the what, when, where, why, and how of the way the hero's problem flared up. Adjusting your trench coat in the mirror, you decide to use your best Columbo charm—and to add "Columbo charm" to your oxymoron collection.

WITNESS REPORT

WITNESS	WHAT HAPPENED	WHERE	WHEN	QUOTES

There are four words you never want to hear Columbo say: "Just one more question ...."

After a lengthy, rambling, and sometimes annoying interview, if you were on the wrong side of a case, you just couldn't wait for Columbo to leave. Just when you thought you were getting him out of your hair, just as he was on his way out the door, perhaps to smoke that stub of a cigar he chewed on but rarely lit, Columbo would turn and say, "Just one more question ...."

If you ever had a hope of holding on to your Get-Out-of-Jail-Free card, Columbo just took away both—your card and your hope.

You may not be locking up any of the characters in the story, but you don't want them holding anything back, either.

ONE MORE QUESTION WORKSHEET

WHO	QUESTION	ANSWER

Back at the office, you hang up your trench coat. All in all, you make a pretty good Columbo. You're starting to enjoy the feel of that unlit pygmy of a cigar dangling from the corner of your mouth. You can see yourself being Columbo for the rest of your life, especially if it would help you avoid the paperwork you hear calling you from the top drawer of your desk.

Columbo was not one for careful record-keeping. (He paid even less attention to rules, regulations, and protocol.) He dodged paperwork the way he dodged trips to the car wash. Yet even Columbo took notes and had to reveal to his higher-ups the details of his investigations. You do, too. Those "certain friends and acquaintances" can be a lot harder on you than the brass ever was on Columbo.

It's time to begin compiling your final report.

Write a short paragraph describing the hero's usual days. Then write another short paragraph describing how his problem upended his daily routine.

FINAL REPORT ENTRY 1

"Is that your report there?" Columbo says, pointing to your notes on your desk. "Would you mind very much if I read what you wrote? I'm a bit of a mystery buff myself." You hand your notes to the lieutenant, thinking about all you've accomplished today.

"This is good. This is very, very good. I see here the hero is already in trouble and doesn't know it. That's a nice start." You smile, wondering if maybe having Columbo help you on this case might be the way to go.

"Just one question," Columbo says. "What happens next?"

Then again …

EXAMPLE

We know Francine is concerned about getting older, but it's not the sort of thing she thinks about constantly. Maybe it pops into her mind when she's surprised by some new ache and pain, or when she has trouble reading a cookbook or hearing what Horace says, but it's far from the first thing on her mind in the morning or the last thing at night. That's a conscious choice. She doesn't want to think about her age and its implications—in fact, she probably goes the other way. She feels young. She looks at the world through young eyes. When she sees a man in his 40s, or even 30s, she flirts. If he doesn't flirt back, she gives nary a thought to the fact that he's not interested because he sees a woman nearing 60. While her world is going one way—getting older—Francine acts and feels as if she's getting younger.

We also know that Francine is upset that Stanley doesn't have a relative in the family that he can be proud of. Along with maintaining her youth, she wants to be that relative, which means she not only needs to make her mark, she needs to make it quickly.

Stories are generally full of conflict, and we shouldn't pass up the chance to add conflict to ours. Here there's conflict between what is (Francine's age) and what isn't (Francine's imagined age). There's also conflict between her making her mark in any old way and making her mark in a way that will make Stanley proud. What sorts of things might crop up repeatedly in Francine's day-to-day life to demonstrate—to herself and others—that she's as young as she ever was and capable of chasing the fame she desires?

DAY-TO-DAY ACTIVITIES

Working out at the gym

Shopping at the health-food store

Exercising at home

Daily jogs through town

Getting facials and spa treatments

Showing off for her nephew

Dancing (with Horace?), rocking out

Doing things with her nephew—soccer, amusement park, lunch

Hanging out with a younger crowd—drinking, dancing

Chaperoning high school dances

Buying clothes at young people's stores

Working as a bartender

Taking community college classes—art, music

Writing a book

Taking acting lessons

Taking high-performance driving lessons

The list is a combination of items that could make her famous (art, music, acting, writing) and pursuits that could keep her perceptually young. We can narrow down the list with the two-step approach (pick three ideas and then the best of the three):

- Writing a book

- Exercising

- Going to the amusement park with Stanley (her nephew)

The exercise entry is a bit of a cheat because it encompasses several list entries, but we can identify some sort of day-to-day exercise routine as part of her regimen. We know something has to happen to Francine to remind her that her make-your-mark clock is ticking.

Writing a book is a nice choice because writing is a route to fame that takes forever and a couple years after that. When whatever happens to Francine happens, she may realize she doesn't have time to wait for publishing magic.

Taking Stanley to the amusement park is not a day-to-day activity, but bumming around with her nephew is. She may not do so in person, but let's say she talks to him all the time via e-mail, the telephone, or Skype. After all, she doesn't have any kids, and she has lots of time on her hands. Francine might very well be a helicopter aunt, especially if her sister isn't a doting or diligent mom.

For something she can work on daily, for something to preoccupy her life and thoughts while she works on making her mark, let's go with writing a book. The other entries on the list may very well be part of her life, and we can use them in other ways later.

Francine is writing a book. We don't know what it's about yet, and that's okay. What's important now is that it's part of her daily routine, and it's also a part of her strategy to make her mark, and make Stanley proud, before it's too late. Picture Francine imagining what's going to happen to her when she's a famous author. How does all this show up in her day-to-day life? Fill out a day-to-day activities worksheet. Here are some representative entries.

DAY-TO-DAY ACTIVITIES WORKSHEET

WHO	WHERE	WHAT	EVENTS OF INTEREST	QUOTES FROM WITNESSES
Horace	coffee shop	yellow pad	writes everywhere	"She's a writing machine."
Carla	hairdresser	voice recorder	writes during movies	"It's annoying."
Sister	in the car	reams of printer paper	writes during dinner	"I don't want that in your book."
Stanley	post office	favorite fountain pen		"Francine? Are you listening?"

With each brain-sleuthing session, Francine becomes more finely drawn. She's emerging as someone who isn't merely writing a book; she's an obsessed individual. Her friends don't share her excitement for the adventure, for it seems the book may be incorporating them into its pages. This didn't turn up in the investigation into Francine's background, but we know it now, and we'll likely use it later.

Francine writes everywhere she goes, but the key here is that she goes places. She does things. While engaged in her writing, something happened to tell her or remind her that the window for finishing her book is closing rapidly. It has to be something dramatic, something she can't ignore (even though she'll try), but not something that totally incapacitates her, because she still has 90 percent of this story to travel through.

There's plenty on her list of daily activities to work with. She's very active, or tries to be, so something could go physically wrong—anything from aches and pains to a (mild) heart attack. One intriguing item on the list is that she regularly interacts with her nephew. He's going to figure into the story, so this may be a good time to involve Francine with Stanley, and vice versa.

The notion that she takes him to the amusement park is different, and sort of encompasses several of Francine's many sides: her quirkiness; her desire to be young, or to stay connected with events that keep her young; and her fondness for Stanley. Suppose Francine takes Stanley to the amusement park and something happens there. With all those whirling and twirling rides, and Francine not being as young as she wants to believe she is, there's the opportunity for trouble. Not *trouble* trouble, but the sort of thing we're looking for. Something that reminds Francine she's a kid at heart, but not of body.

The hero was ___riding amusement park rides___ *when* ___she got dizzy and threw up___ .

This may not be the whole story, but it's a good starting point. We can imagine Francine trying to keep up with Stanley, overdoing it, and getting a slap in the face from reality.

Francine overdid it and paid for it—in public, and especially in front of Stanley. But what happened exactly? We have the general idea; now we need to fill in the specifics.

FIELD REPORT WORKSHEET

PEOPLE	PLACES	EVENTS WORTH NOTING
roller-coaster operator	Tilt-a-Whirl exit	pool of vomit by Tilt-a-Whirl ride (contains traces of corn dogs, cotton candy, and banana smoothie)
various parents and kids	smoothie stand	tracks in sand show stumbling, hesitation
couple in front seat of ride	Tilt-a-Whirl exit	damp paper towels scattered about in front of ride
corn dog stand kid	corn dog stand	blood on grass
smoothie shack kid	Spinning Mushroom ride	little kids fascinated with vomit pool
guy in Danger Dog suit	popcorn stand	
security guard	dime pitching booth	flashing ambulance lights
paramedic	softball throw	bells, horns, sirens
obnoxious lady with child	Tilt-a-Whirl exit	wants her money back

Filling out the worksheet helps convert the general idea of throwing up at the amusement park into something specific. Two points emerge: Francine not only overdid the park rides, but she also tried to keep up with Stanley's youthful eating habits.

What also emerged is that the scene feels more like a carnival or county fair than a slick, Disney-like mega-entertainment production. This wasn't necessarily the plan going in, but it makes sense given that Stanley lives in a small community. Perhaps going to carnivals and fairs is one of the bonding activities she and Stanley share. In any event, throwing up at a smaller venue, in the company of people Stanley and his mother undoubtedly see every day, makes the situation much worse for Francine. As we know, making things worse for the hero is what stories do.

The combination of keeping up with Stanley's taste in rides and fine dining created a more-than-embarrassing situation for Francine. We've already noticed the tracks in the sand, the blood on the grass, and of course the vomit. We're getting a picture of what happened, but some details are still missing. Here are some representative entries from the witness report, followed by some Columbo-style one last questions.

WITNESS REPORT

WITNESS	WHAT HAPPENED	WHERE	WHEN	QUOTES
ride operator	the old lady barfed	by the exit	right after she got off the ride	"The whole thing stinks. It's bad for business."
obnoxious lady with kid	she came at me waving her arms and then threw up	right in front of me		"She should act her age."
paramedic	overeating, indi-gestion, excessive visual stimulation and disorientation, she fell and her head struck a rock	just north of the exit gate, in the grass	apparently after eating, but was probably sick on the ride	"I think she didn't realize she's not 15 anymore."

ONE MORE QUESTION WORKSHEET

WHO	QUESTION	ANSWER
ride operator	What if I told you she was perfectly healthy and that it was your ride that made her sick?	"I'd say you didn't see her trying to do somersaults on the grass over there with her kid."
obnoxious lady with kid	Have you ever done something embarrassing in front of your kid?	"Yes. Talked to you. I'm sorry. Maybe the woman was just having fun."
paramedic	Don't you think it's a little strange she slipped and hit her head on what appears to be the only rock for 20 feet in any direction?	"Yes, I do."

Francine may have put on quite a show after getting off the Tilt-a-Whirl, a show that encompassed dizziness, incoherence, and a bit of stumbling, followed by a very public display of her stomach's contents. We can pretty much see the picture of her overdoing it, probably for a couple hours before the Tilt-a-Whirl delivered the coup de grâce. The ride operator let us know she was putting on quite an exhibition of her youthfulness. The obnoxious lady admitted Francine seemed to be enjoying herself. There's some question as to whether she actually hit her head, perhaps. It's a nice detail, and only time will tell whether it's relevant to the story. At this point of the process, though, it's best not to throw away anything.

This chapter's previous worksheets, along with what we've uncovered from our investigation of Francine, contain enough information, when helped along by some imagination, to create the opening moments of the story, as expressed in the first entry of our final report. The trick is to be brief but descriptive.

It's easy to get swept away by rambling or, going the other way, to write terse descriptions that are a hair more illuminating than bullet points. Some tips from other story detectives may help you:

- Think visually, and see the people, places, and actions before you write them down.

- Use a detective's eye and highlight unusual details or things that seem out of place.

- Remember to answer who, what, when, where, why, and how.

- Choose verbs and adjectives that minimize the lengths of sentences while making it easier to visualize what you're describing.

FINAL REPORT ENTRY 1

At 58, Francine feels time is her enemy. Every week she works out, watches her diet, and tries to rekindle the spark of youthful romance with her husband, Horace. But since embarrassing her nephew, Stanley, while speaking at his school's career day, Francine has been obsessed with writing a book. Vowing to give Stanley a relative he can be proud of, she works on her book constantly, much to the consternation of her friends, associates, and strangers, who find her making notes, dictating into her voice recorder, and asking them strange—and mostly annoying—questions quite irritating. But for Francine, it is her last chance to, as she put it, accomplish something she could be proud of.

Taking a break from book authorship, Francine heads to Idaho to visit Stanley and takes her nephew to the county fair. Demonstrating her youthfulness, she matches Stanley corn dog for corn dog, cotton candy for cotton candy, and scary ride for scary ride. It is after the Tilt-a-Whirl, though, that the spinning scenery, flashing lights, and random diet finally claim her as a victim. Exiting the ride, Francine stumbles, spins around, and, before falling to the ground, leaves the vivid, yellow-green tinged details of everything she's eaten all over the midway lawn.

For some added interest, and urgency, we've included a sentence about Francine embarrassing Stanley in front of his classmates. We can imagine how that might go. Stanley is picked on because he comes from a line of boring people and Francine, his savior, is just as boring, talking about her job in the post office punching in the first three digits of ZIP codes. After humiliating Stanley, she has even more of a reason to become famous. We'll use that reason to add drive to the story.

Chapter 10

The Case of the Daily Denial

To a story detective, cause and effect are better than that first sip of morning coffee after a night that went on too long and ended with your going home alone. When it comes to understanding cause and effect, nobody does it better than Gil Grissom.

Ask Grissom about the details of a bus accident outside Las Vegas, and he'll hand you a report with drawings, pictures, and paragraphs laying out a series of actions and reactions, and causes and effects that led to the fatal crash. A vengeful former bus company employee puts chloroform in the bus's right front tire. Somewhere between Barstow, California, and Las Vegas, the tire comes apart. The driver overcompensates. The suspension system gets stressed out. A substandard bolt snaps in two. The rod arm it's holding up breaks. The bus sideswipes a Camaro. The end.

"For every action, there's an equal and opposite reaction," Grissom would tell you in his matter-of-fact way. For Grissom, worshipping at the feet of Sir Isaac Newton is better than a week of Hail Mary's.

Grissom relies on the laws of physics to track his causes and effects. As a story detective, you have to put your faith in the laws of human physics. They're less reliable, and they're sometimes unpredictable, but people are still people and heroes are still heroes. Push them hard enough one way, and they're going to push back in the other.

Like the chloroform in the tire, the hero's problem began small. Although the result might not have been a fatal crash, you can bet the hero was heading for a catastrophe. Right now, though, you have to figure out what the hero did. You know the cause. What is the effect?

For an answer to that question, you ask Grissom about another law of physics: a body at rest remains at rest. In hero terms, a body at rest wants to stay in bed or in a chair with its feet up on the desk. The average Joe wants to stay lost in his cup of joe for as long as he can manage it. The only people looking for change stand on street corners with paper cups.

Sure, things have changed. That's what happens in heroes' lives. But like the bus hurtling down the highway, it took more than one event to move the hero in anything but a straight line. Now that the hero's been reminded of his problem, do some brain-sleuthing and uncover how he avoided what he knew he has to deal with.

HERO AVOIDS PROBLEM

WHAT HERO IS NEWLY AWARE OF	WHAT HERO DOES TO AVOID PROBLEM

With any luck, you've probably got a list of variations on a theme—the hero kept on doing what he was doing, only he worked harder at it just to prove to himself—and to you, if you get close enough—there was nothing wrong. The tire blew, and the driver just overcompensated for it. Look over your list and see what the hero did to jerk the steering wheel to keep on a straight-line course.

HERO MAINTAINS A STRAIGHT LINE

WHAT DOES HE DO	WHERE	OBJECTIVE	WHO ELSE IS INVOLVED

It should be no surprise that Grissom believes not only in the laws of science, but also in the importance of the written word. You should, too. Time to commit your findings to paper. If you aren't sure of the details yet, of how the hero brushed aside his problem and pretended all is well, Grissom would tell you to return to the field, scour the scene for more evidence, prepare another field report, and interview more witnesses. When you're ready, write it up in your final report. Devote two or three sentences to each step the hero took to prove to the world—and himself—that his life is normal.

FINAL REPORT ENTRY 2

The cause and effect chain has started rolling. The laws of human physics have nudged you on your way, but action-reaction, things don't stop here. If they did, you could report to those voices in your head that the hero lived out his life without anything else of note happening and there's no point in continuing to eyeball him under a microscope as if he were something scraped off those fuzzy-looking leftovers in the back of the fridge. As a good story detective, you know things are going to get worse for the hero. You even know how. Grissom found out the tire that caused the bus accident didn't blow out by itself—it had help.

The hero's woes have help, too. That's what the bad guys are for.

We can assume Francine is both shaken and resolute after her little adventure at the county fair. She's not going to see this as a sign she needs to slow down. She's far more likely to rationalize the whole sordid affair.

HERO AVOIDS PROBLEM

WHAT HERO IS NEWLY AWARE OF	WHAT HERO DOES TO AVOID PROBLEM
getting old	gives up and grows old
time is running out	acts her age
people know she's not as young as she used to be	gets more exercise begins stricter diet
options are narrowing	pretends nothing's wrong takes another trip to the fair speeds up everything, does everything faster hires a trainer hires a life coach looks for shortcut for writing her book takes up something with a faster payoff like donating money takes a writing class

What's forced its way into Francine's consciousness is the idea that time is running out (if she's at all honest with herself). Rather than dramatically changing her plan, Francine tweaks it a little. But mostly, she stays on the same path toward making her mark.

If Francine doesn't do anything different, she's in danger of becoming a rather uninteresting hero. On the other hand, she's still in that denial/ignorance zone, so her reaction will probably be somewhat muted. (She's not going to throw away everything she's done and embark on a wild new plan to make her mark—not while she still believes she can avoid making any major changes.) More than likely, she'll just speed up what she's doing and rationalize her actions by telling others, and herself, that she just wants to throw herself into her work and that she's excited about what she's doing. She wants to get her book out there right away because it will inspire so many people or because it's a story that simply must be told.

HERO MAINTAINS A STRAIGHT LINE

WHAT DOES HE DO	WHERE	OBJECTIVE	WHO ELSE IS INVOLVED
goes running	usual streets	proves there's nothing wrong	fellow runners to whom she brags about how good she feels
doubles hours spent writing	locked in her bedroom	doesn't want somebody to beat her to writing her book	Horace, indirectly by being ignored by Francine
borrows money to donate	local bank	be remembered by putting your name on something	Horace the bank loan officer the bank president

The notion from the previous worksheet that she might want to donate money is worth thinking about because it's a little off center from Francine's book writing, but it's still in line with Francine's goal. Francine wants to make her mark—it's the whole point of writing the book. But what if writing the book suddenly seems impractical?

Fame and recognition are both everlasting monuments one can erect by, say, having a library or college building named after you. If not a whole building, a meeting room, a museum gallery, or a theater lobby maybe. The idea of donating money also has some resonance with banks, and Francine will be robbing them down the line. Perhaps this is the moment her bank-robbing plans begin taking shape.

FINAL REPORT ENTRY 2

Back home the next day, and despite her doctor's orders, Francine goes for her usual morning run. Not only does she double-time it, she makes a point of telling virtually everyone she passes—nearly a dozen startled runners and twice as many passers-by—that she is in the best shape ever.

For the next few weeks, Francine seems to shut herself off from the rest of the world. She works longer and longer hours. Horace jokes that he doesn't have a wife and begins calling Francine his "boarder." Oblivious, Francine cranks out page after page of her book as if racing some competing, imaginary author toward an equally imaginary finish line.

If Francine never rises above her denial the story will come to a halt. We know there's something on the horizon that will bring her face to face with reality. That's where our sleuthing will take us next—after we take a brief detour to identify an obstacle standing between Francine and her making her mark.

Chapter 11

The Case of the Second Story

You're thumbing through your wallet, looking for the emergency $20 you stash behind your credit card—the card that's only good these days for shimming open your front door when you forget your keys. Instead, you come across an old business card from Thomas Banacek.

Banacek is the kind of detective we all want to be. Not that he lists them on his business card, but he's intelligent, resourceful, creative, and rich. At least that's the talk when good gumshoes get together to toss back a few while trading stories.

While he has a knack for solving impossible crimes, Banacek also has a knack for dropping the hammer on the wrong suspects. At least that's what they say while being led out of the room in bright, shiny bracelets.

Banacek rarely pinches a perp who says, "Thank God you caught me. I've been a bad person." That millionaire's beautiful assistant didn't say it when Banacek sent her to the slammer for stealing her boss's prized rare book. Neither did the owner of Cap'n Jack's Clam Bakeries who stole $5 million in stock certificates from the company that bought him out.

Not that Banacek asked you, but as a story detective, you know there's a perfectly rational explanation for this type of criminal behavior.

Every bad guy is a good guy in his own story.

The millionaire's assistant, well she had the book coming—once she found out she wasn't in her boss's will. "All that time and not one stupid penny," she said to Banacek about her years of employment. "It wasn't fair. He stole seven years out of my life. For a lie."

And Cap'n Jack? His tale of woe was that he wouldn't be getting a hefty monthly expense check from the new owners of his restaurants. He was about to go back to his old penny ante life, and he didn't deserve that.

Every bad guy is a good guy in his own story.

If you're going to make sense of this case, you're going to have to find out who the villain is and put his story together, too, just as you put together the hero's once-upon-a-time scenario.

Not that the villain's story will always paint him or her as the Darth Vader of storytelling. The villain could be some sweet old lady who doesn't even know she's wandered into the hero's way. The villain might even be another part of the hero himself, some dark part of his upbringing, some bad experience, his misguided youth, some long-forgotten fear of success, or just some really bad habit. If the hero is his own villain, there's something in him he's got to overcome to be a decent person.

Whoever the villain is, you can be sure of two things. The villain wants something—as badly as the hero wants to solve his problem—and whatever plan the villain has in mind is in direct conflict with the hero's plan. You can put "they both can't win" in the same group as death and taxes.

THE VILLAIN JUST MIGHT BE

WHO	BECAUSE

Do the "certain friends and acquaintances" suspect the hero is on that list? If so, pretend that part of the hero—the part that's unknowingly working against himself—is its own person while you whittle down the list.

The villain I've got to keep my eye on is _____, *and he wants*

_____ .

This is a problem for the hero because _____

_____ .

You can be sure the villain is going to upset the hero's plans, forcing him to zig when he wants to zag, or the other way around. This means that if you're stalking the hero, you'll be stalking the villain as well. Or the other way around.

In either case, now that you're stalking two people, maybe you should talk to those "certain friends and acquaintances" about a bump in that "remuneration commensurate with results." Or maybe you should just lay out some plans for keeping tabs on the villain.

You're going to pull a Jessica Fletcher on the villain's friends, acquaintances, relatives, and hangers-on. Interviews. Stories. A dossier. The whole story detective package.

USUAL SUSPECTS

NOT-SO-USUAL SUSPECTS

INTERVIEWEES

INTERVIEW WORKSHEET

INTERVIEWEE _____

QUESTION	ANSWER

Copy as many times as necessary.

VILLAIN PROFILE SUMMARY

BEHAVIOR	EXAMPLE (WHAT, WHEN, WHERE, WHO)
Frustration	
Anger	
Disappointment	
Decision-making	

BEHAVIOR	EXAMPLE (WHAT, WHEN, WHERE, WHO)
Relationships	
(Add more categories of your own)	

VILLAIN'S NAME _____

EARLY YEARS (where born, raised to age 13, give or take)

TEEN YEARS (school, growing up, dating)

ADULT YEARS (jobs, career, plans, life)

PRESENT (last month before case started)

ADDITIONAL INFO (weaknesses, fears, vulnerabilities, strengths)

FRIENDS/HELPERS INTERVIEW WORKSHEET

INTERVIEWEE _____

QUESTION	ANSWER

Copy as many times as necessary.

FRIEND/HELPER'S NAME _____

EARLY YEARS (where born, raised to age 13, give or take)

TEEN YEARS (school, growing up, dating)

ADULT YEARS (jobs, career, plans, life)

PRESENT (last month before case started)

ADDITIONAL INFO (weaknesses, fears, vulnerabilities, strengths)

VILLAIN'S SKILLS WORKSHEET

SKILL	HOW MIGHT HELP

Time to call it a day—more like a week of long days—and head for home. Hopefully you have your keys. Until you crack this case and score a check, that credit card is going to be thin.

E X A M P L E

It's easy to imagine dealing with a villain who has his sights set on the hero. The robber who's after the cop on his trail, the brother out to deter his sibling who's pursuing a mutual love interest, or the politician bent on destroying the reporter who's out to topple him. In these cases, the interests of the hero and of the villain directly collide, but not all stories are so black and white. Sometimes, the hero and the villain are headed in their own directions, unaware that their paths are tangled.

Who's the villain in this story? Because Francine robs banks, a police officer or FBI agent deserves a place on our list. After that, we might as well add some of the story characters we already know about.

THE VILLAIN JUST MIGHT BE

WHO	BECAUSE
Carla	doesn't want Francine wasting her life
FBI	Francine robbed a bank, or tried to
Local police	Francine robbed a bank, or tried to
Francine	deep down she doesn't want to be famous

Joan	sibling rivalry
Horace	he's an artist, and artists should be famous, too

Horace seems out of place. That's excellent—out-of-place characters and odd situations often lead to interesting stories. Horace hardly seems like the evil, villainous type. He's an artist and artists often become famous. Sometimes they strive for it; sometimes fame finds them. The idea of a husband and wife competing for fame sounds like an idea rife with conflict. We just might have a classic hero/villain situation: two people who are on a collision course.

Remember, it's not necessary for the villain to be mean or despicable. *Villain* is just a convenient term we're using for the character who gets in the way of the hero solving his problem. With Horace yearning for fame, the husband/wife relationship can easily become competitive.

The villain I've got to keep my eye on is ___Horace___ , and he wants ___to pursue and perhaps sell his art___ . This is a problem for the hero because ___they could both be vying for fame___ .

We already have a dossier started on Horace, so we don't have to create one from scratch. Let's add some information to it, based on interviews with his parents and his boss, that will shed some light on his background appropriate for his new role as villain.

VILLAIN'S NAME _____ _Horace_ _____

EARLY YEARS (where born, raised to age 13, give or take)

As a child, Horace's favorite word in social situations was "no."
From an early age, he didn't enjoy socializing, especially in large
groups. It wasn't that he was rebellious; it was more that he was
shy and retiring. He was the sort of youngster who had to be
persuaded or cajoled into mingling with others. Once he took the
first few steps toward socializing, however, he usually enjoyed
himself thoroughly.

TEEN YEARS (school, growing up, dating)

Horace's first recorded kiss—there may have been others—
occurred when he was 13 while at a birthday party for Linda, one
of his classmates. It was not Horace's idea. Not only did he have
to be prodded by his parents to attend the party in the first
place, Linda's mother had to practically drag him out of her
bedroom, where he was hiding behind the bed, sketching animals
on scraps of paper he'd rescued from the trash can. Then, it was
up to Linda to drag Horace out back for that kiss and then drag
him back inside for birthday cake, which he protested he didn't
want. Years later, Horace remembered the day fondly, as one
of the high points of his life. He didn't remember, or he refused
to remember, how reluctant he was to attend the party in the
first place.

ADULT YEARS (jobs, career, plans, life)

Horace's distaste for large groups continued into his adult
years. He often hid out in unused rooms and corners of the
button shop while working on his designs, and his boss had to
practically threaten to fire Horace to get him to attend Fashion
Week events every year. Horace would employ any and all excuses
he could think of, but once he arrived at an event or party,
always with Francine at his side, he enjoyed himself immensely
(although he stopped short of saying he was looking forward to
doing it again).

We have a picture of Horace as someone who—among his other qualities—isn't fond of socializing, especially in large groups. He's not the kind of person who would seek out fame, although apparently he would enjoy it, and its trappings, if it found him.

Horace is not exactly the image of a dastardly villain with a handlebar mustache, but he's certainly in a position to play the villain's role. With his own desire to be recognized for his art, a desire he may not know he has, he and Francine can easily find themselves competing for fame and fortune.

Chapter 12

The Case of the Doomed Denial

Time to get back on the hero's trail. You may not know where he is right now, but you know where he squandered his time. You borrow your brother-in-law's minivan and set the GPS for the corner of Deep and Denial.

The area is empty now, but you can imagine the hero leaning against the lamppost on the corner. And even though the hero may have enjoyed the view, you know he couldn't stay there forever, no more than one of House's patients could stay cuddled comfortably in a bed enjoying the hospital's haute cuisine.

House, in fact, counts on it. While his patients are denying they drank duplicating fluid, had unprotected sex, took drugs, or have ever been sick a day in their lives, what's eating them away on the inside is clawing its way to the outside. It's only a matter of time until the symptoms are in need of more attention than a cat waiting for its evening meal.

The only question on House's mind is how long that's going to take. For the hero, you know the answer was, "Not long." The hero's already self-medicated himself by doing whatever he's been doing to demonstrate to the world, and himself, that there's nothing wrong, nothing out of the ordinary, nothing about his life that he can't handle.

Now, like House, you want to enjoy this moment of realization, though probably without House's smug grin.

You know what that moment was. Peggy pointed you toward it. You brain-sleuthed it out when you decided the hero was a worthy client and not about to walk out of the story on you. What was that event, the one the hero couldn't ignore?

The hero can't ignore that _____

_____

_____.

Chances are, it's not just one thing but a series of things, a string of causes and effects that forced the hero into taking an action. What are they? What two or three causes forced the hero to confess something was wrong and something needed to be done?

HERO'S END OF DENIAL

SOME LIKELY CAUSES OF HERO'S END OF DENIAL

AND SOME UNLIKELY ONES

BUT OUT OF THEM ALL, THE TWO OR THREE MOST LIKELY

When House is faced with denials, he merely casts them aside. Okay, he berates and ridicules the patient first but then he casts aside the denials. House sees denials as hospital gowns covering up clues. From the front denials cover everything. But when you get behind them, denials are not hiding much at all.

It's your turn to see what the denials have been hiding. Get out in the field and take a look. Fill out a field report for each event that led up to the problem the hero couldn't ignore.

FIELD REPORT WORKSHEET

PEOPLE	PLACES	EVENTS WORTH NOTING

WITNESS REPORT

WITNESS	WHAT HAPPENED	WHERE	WHEN	QUOTES

House has to write up case notes for Cuddy, or bully Foreman or Chase into doing it for him. You can do the same, but you'll have to bully yourself. Review your field report, and add the causes to your final report. Give this entry a short paragraph.

FINAL REPORT ENTRY 3

That lamppost is still deserted, waiting for its next hero. Your hero has moved on. You'd better do the same. Your brother-in-law's minivan? He's charging you by the hour.

E X A M P L E

At the beginning of the case, we discovered that Francine felt the pressure of time robbing her of the opportunity to make her mark, to be remembered for something.

The hero can't ignore that __she's getting older and time is__ __running out__ .

Something happens that forces Francine's hand. Chances are, it's not just one thing but a series of causes and events that lead up to a moment Francine can no longer ignore.

HERO'S END OF DENIAL

SOME LIKELY CAUSES OF HERO'S END OF DENIAL

She's running out of money.

She can't find anyone to publish her book.

It's taking longer than she thought to write her book.

She can't seem to get a handle on the book's content.

She gets sick.

Horace gets sick.

AND SOME UNLIKELY ONES

Stanley calls her old.

Carla points out how old she is.

They're about to lose the house.

BUT OUT OF THEM ALL, THE TWO OR THREE MOST LIKELY

The book takes longer than she thought.

She's running out of money.

They're about to lose the house.

While all these ideas are workable, one of the secrets behind a good story is that the hero gets deeper into trouble, usually by his own hand as opposed to the arbitrariness of fate. When uncovering what happens next, it's often a good idea to pick situations the hero can't wriggle out of. Finding out nobody wants to buy her book could be one such event for Francine. News like that would be devastating to anyone with a dream—although if Francine were persistent, she might still prevail.

On the other hand, if she and Horace are running out of money, that problem is a bit harder to solve. It's also a situation an obsessed, self-absorbed person like Francine could find herself in. Suppose Francine leaves her job for the few months she decides it will take her to pound out her tome. It's easy to imagine her ignoring others who say it could take years to finish a book. Remember, when we compiled her dossier, we uncovered her penchant for my-way-or-the-highway behavior.

In that dossier, we have Francine retired from the post office, but now we see that we still want her employed. At any point in the story detective process, we make the best decisions we can based on what we know. If it turns out a choice doesn't work, we make a different one. Francine needs to be employed, so we'll simply change her dossier to reflect that.

It's fine for Francine and Horace to run out of money, but it's even worse if they run out of money and find they're at risk of losing their house. As story detectives, we look cynically for the worst in any situation. From a story perspective, being on the verge of living on the street is much better than watching a bank account spiral down to empty.

By now you should have the flow of visiting the scene of an event, interviewing witnesses, and collecting evidence. To save time—not to mention pages of examples that probably won't be all that illuminating—let's skip detailed field report examples and explain, when necessary, what inspired the information in the final report entries.

Francine and Horace can find out they're about to lose the house in several ways. A letter from the bank is likely the most direct way of discovery, but what could make things even worse? Francine confronting the bank manager in person, perhaps? This scene has an advantage, too. We know Francine will eventually rob a bank. Here's an opportunity for her to build up some anger and resentment toward her future target.

While interviewing witnesses, we learn Francine put on quite a show when the bank manager told her there was nothing he could do to forestall the foreclosure proceedings. Many people described her antics as nothing short of a temper tantrum.

FINAL REPORT ENTRY 3

Francine takes a short leave of absence from the post office in order to pound out her book without distractions. Many months—and several emergency home and car repairs later—Horace and Francine are nearly out of money. When the bank notifies them their mortgage is in default, Francine meets with the manager to reason with him. One word leads to another, and Francine throws a temper tantrum right in the middle of the bank. Nobody knows what to do. The customers all turn away and ignore her. The guard, an unarmed kid who doesn't seem *to know if it is okay to physically restrain a female customer, is helpless. Eventually, everyone is relieved when Francine storms out.*

It seems now our story is shifting into gear. Francine has undergone a brutal reality check and, more important, she did something about it. She took an action. We'll have to wait to see what effect that action had.

Chapter 13

The Case of the Back-and-Forth Battle

It's another one of those days when the last thing on your mind is the case. It's starting to feel like all the other cases you've had, with the long-suffering hero denying the obvious and those "certain friends and acquaintances" expecting you to follow the hero around while he mutters, "Woe is me."

All of which makes it the perfect time to scan the crime pages in the morning paper and read about the mysterious disappearance of a revolutionary new automobile—along with the railroad flatcar it's riding on—from a nonstop train. Or maybe you'll find a story about a race horse switcheroo in which a prize thoroughbred is replaced by an old nag in the middle of a workout lap. Not that you'd ever catch a case like that. Those are the kinds of cases that wind up in the lap of Thomas Banacek.

But there's no reason you can't dream about it.

When you stop dreaming and wake up, it's not only time for your morning coffee break, but you realize Banacek's detective style is what you need to jump-start this case. Banacek's the sort of guy who's more at home in a swordfight than a fistfight—not that he can't lay out somebody with a couple rights and a left. He's done both at once, decking a guy in a powdered wig and nineteenth-century clothing after defeating him with a sword.

The point is, Banacek is more of a thrust-and-parry kind of guy. Whether it's swords or chess or a battle of wits, Banacek favors a back-and-forth, give-and-take battle to a quick kick to the groin or a frying pan over the head. Sometimes he pushes forward and sometimes he gives a bit to gain an advantage.

The hero worked the story that way, too.

As much as the hero would have liked to make a beeline for the finish line and get this whole, sordid problem-solving and life-changing mess into the record books, he couldn't. By accident or on purpose, he kept running into the villain. Sure, the villain would have liked to simply jump straight to world domination, or whatever it was he was looking for, but he kept crossing swords with the hero. Sometimes the hero charged ahead. Sometimes he backed up and figured out a different move.

You know what happened to the hero. He came to the realization that he had to do something. He could no longer deny he had a problem. He needed to take a step—call it a thrust—in the direction of solving his problem. He needed to do it quickly because he sensed what you already knew, that things were going downhill.

The hero thought he could head things off. Too bad he didn't know how impossible that was going to be.

Right now, you'd settle for finding out what the hero's thrust—his first move—was. To do that, you've got to think like the old hero—the hero who's holed up in that dossier on your desk. You thumb through the pages to remind yourself of what the hero has to work with, how he handles problems and makes decisions. Maybe there's a similar problem in the hero's past, a time when he was standing on that very same corner of Deep and Denial. What strategy did he use then? How might he have adapted it to his new situation? What other behaviors might he have fallen back on to get himself out of this mess? What does your brain-sleuthing tell you about the options the hero might consider?

HERO'S FIRST MOVE

THE HERO MIGHT

OR EVEN

OR SURPRISE EVERYONE AND COME UP WITH

As long as this is your Banacek-style case, there's no reason not to head into the field in Banacek style. Like him, you instruct your driver to take you to the scene of the action, where the hero makes his first move. Okay, your driver isn't wearing a black chauffeur's cap, there's a hack license posted on the back of the front seat, and your driver's car is a cheery yellow instead of a somber black. Still, you can always dream.

FIELD REPORT WORKSHEET

PEOPLE	PLACES	EVENTS WORTH NOTING

WITNESS REPORT

WITNESS	WHAT HAPPENED	WHERE	WHEN	QUOTES

While your driver is on a well-earned (according to him) bathroom break, take a few minutes to update your final report with a paragraph on the hero's first move.

FINAL REPORT ENTRY 4

As long as you've got your driver at your disposal—and that's as long as you're willing to watch the meter run—you might as well head over to the scene of the villain's first move. This could have been the first move of his own story, taken without any knowledge of what the hero did. Or the villain may have known full well what was on the hero's mind and moved to shut him down. Either way, the villain's action made it harder for the hero to solve his problem.

VILLAIN'S FIRST MOVE

THE VILLAIN MIGHT

OR EVEN

OR SURPRISE EVERYONE AND COME UP WITH

Which first move did you select? Get the details by scouring the scene.

FIELD REPORT WORKSHEET

PEOPLE	PLACES	EVENTS WORTH NOTING

WITNESS REPORT

WITNESS	WHAT HAPPENED	WHERE	WHEN	QUOTES

By the time you open the door to your office and plop down at your desk, your yellow limo has vanished and you're feeling more like a post-midnight Cinderella than an end-of-the-day Banacek with his brandy and cigar. Banacek, it seems, never had to write down any of his case details. He just related them with that if-you're-so-smart-how-come-you-had-to-hire-me? grin of his. But after his brandy—or maybe because of it—he didn't have to answer to those "certain friends and acquaintances" either.

You pull out your final report and write another short paragraph. Then you can call it a night, get some well-deserved rest, and imagine that next time you'll get a real Banacek case.

Hey, you can always dream.

FINAL REPORT ENTRY 5

EXAMPLE

Sometimes you'll have to search for the hero's first move, and sometimes it'll be right there waiting for you. Francine's story appears to be an example of the latter. Sooner or later, Francine is going to rob a bank. This certainly seems like the time. To be on the safe side, though, let's brain-sleuth some other possibilities.

HERO'S FIRST MOVE

THE HERO MIGHT

Rob a bank.

Return to work at the post office.

Find another job.

Give up her dream.

Borrow the money she needs.

Sell off possessions.

OR EVEN

Steal.

Sell drugs.

OR SURPRISE EVERYONE AND COME UP WITH

Sell pencils on street corners.

Sell watches on street corners.

Run a street corner scam.

We can cross out some ideas almost instantly. Giving up on her dream brings the story to an end, and we've already convinced ourselves Francine isn't walking out on us. Borrowing the money only prolongs the inevitable. She borrows money, she writes, and she runs out of money. Whoops, we're back where we started. Writers call this dancing in place because the events do nothing to advance the story. We only need to have Francine run out of money once to keep moving forward.

The other ideas call on Francine to do something illegal. A self-fulfilling prophesy perhaps, but it's where we knew this story was heading. More importantly, robbing a bank makes sense in the context of what we've uncovered. Francine is angry at the bank, and she added an important element to her resource list when she met with the bank manager. Call it knowledge or experience, but Francine learned that if you create enough confusion, nobody will know what to do.

Robbing a bank lets us move the story forward using characters and situations we're already working with. That's usually the best choice to make. As always, if we run into trouble we can revisit the decision.

We've tacitly assumed this story plays out in the present day, but robbing a bank—let alone setting off any kind of explosion—in a post–September 11 world is no longer an act of misguided mischief. Instead, it would be met with a response that's not in keeping with the lighthearted quality of this story. We need to tell this tale in a simpler world at a simpler time, a time before bullet-proof teller cages and the Department of Homeland Security.

Changing the era in which the story occurs is a perfectly legal choice. As a story detective, you're free to revisit, and alter, any and all of your decisions. In this case, let's set the story in the early 1970s, when banks were small and regional and people could walk around the lobby without arousing suspicion. Nothing in our story so far is time-dependent, so nothing needs changed. In preparing our final report, we just need to be sure we establish our choice of time frame.

From the field interviews with the bank manager, the guard, and the bank customers (a mix of men and women, mothers with their children, and wives with their husbands), we get the details of what happened. The bank was crowded, Francine was in disguise, and the addition to the final report describes it all.

FINAL REPORT ENTRY 4

Carla's offhand comment that Francine should return to the post office or start robbing banks is all the encouragement she needs. A few days later, heavily disguised and wrapped in a fur coat, Francine walks into the crowded bank. She quietly places a small package next to a potted plant and waits in an agonizingly slow line for a teller. In front of the teller, Francine opens her coat to reveal she is stark naked. People gasp. Mothers cover their children's eyes. Men stare as their wives hit them over the head with shopping bags. Francine demands all the money to cover herself back up. As before, nobody knows quite what to do. Suddenly, and somewhat prematurely, a loud bang comes from the vicinity of the potted plant, and creamed corn spews everywhere. An angry and empty-handed Francine darts out the back door. When the police arrive on the scene, all the witnesses can agree on, at least the male witnesses, is that she had <u>some</u> body.

Meanwhile, Horace is on a path that's going to make him famous. Maybe he didn't seek it out, but when it happens, he certainly doesn't shy away from it. It sounds as if we know Horace's first move. He accepts his newfound fame. What we now need to uncover is how he got famous. Even though this step is about brain-sleuthing the villain's first move, we need to be flexible and open story detectives. Sometimes we'll know the step but not why it happened. Sometimes we'll have a general idea of what happened but not the specifics. Sometimes we'll be thrashing around trying to get a handle on both. Our job is to put our story detective skills to work at each step to uncover what we need to know.

VILLAIN'S FIRST MOVE

There's a sudden interest in exploding cans of vegetables in the art community.

Horace promotes his art more actively because of the bank incident.

It's the era of pop art, and Horace's art just suddenly clicks.

Horace's work is discovered by a famous artist.

Horace has always been mildly famous, and now his time has come.

Horace changes galleries, and the new gallery is better at promoting his work than the previous one.

Horace meets an art critic and charms her.

On very special occasions, the idea you're looking for will come marching up the street trailed by a brass band. When that happens, don't critique the music or ask the band if it can play "When the Saints Go Marching In." Welcome the idea into the story, and move on.

There's little need to brain-sleuth here. Horace makes art, which apparently nobody wants, by exploding cans of vegetables and then documenting the results on canvas. Francine borrows the exploding can of vegetables to cover her escape. News of the robbery attempt stimulates an interest in Horace's art, and suddenly Horace is rescued from obscurity.

FINAL REPORT ENTRY 5

Word of the strange doings in the bank generate buzz, and shortly thereafter, the owner of the gallery where Horace has a few of his paintings on consignment calls. Horace's work sold out, at excellent prices. Could he and Francine come to New York City? A reporter for the <u>Times</u> wants to do a story on him. And how quickly can he make more art?

After a successful trip to New York, Horace and Francine return home with enough money to forestall the foreclosure and allow Francine to return to her writing. When Francine describes the trip to Carla, Carla observes that Francine didn't seem as happy as she should be about this turn of events.

The story, to paraphrase a well-worn phrase, thickens. Horace, who has toiled in relative obscurity, is no longer Francine's obscure relative. For her, the story has taken an unexpected turn and provided another link in the cause-and-effect chain.

Chapter 14

The Case of the Hero's Loose Change

You've been following the hero for what feels like halfway through the case, and you're still waiting for the big change those "certain friends and acquaintances" have been complaining about. "There came a time," they say with increasing insistence, "that he just wasn't himself. That is, he was himself, but he wasn't. Not all the time."

The story detective game would be a great racket, you think, *if only we could get rid of the clients.*

This time, though, you catch their drift. If you were on better terms with them, you'd introduce them to another detective, Jim Rockford—not that you're looking to foist them off on some other unsuspecting gumshoe. You've got too much invested in this case to let some other PI grab any of the glory.

It's just that right now, based on what those "certain friends and acquaintances" are telling you, the hero is looking less like a hero and more like a Rockford. Rockford is a savvy, somewhat successful guy, but you always wondered if he'd be able to break free of his shady past. Now you've got the same question about the hero.

Okay, maybe the hero's past isn't shady, but up until now, he's been stuck to it like white on rice, the way Rockford goes arm-in-arm with con games, ex-cons, and future ex-cons. Rockford may be trying to leave all that behind, pick up a little cash, and rack up enough free hours for fishing, but scratch below the surface of any of Rockford's cases, and you can't slip a sheet of paper between him and his questionable background. Whether he's selling a friend's business to the mob, drilling for oil in the middle of a condominium complex driveway, or heading to the beach at sunset for a leisurely car chase along the sand, Rockford's attempts at breaking away from the old days only seem to pull him back in.

The villain's latest move served only to make things worse for the hero, just the way some thug spoils Rockford's dinner by shoving a .45 in his ribs—and not the ribs on his plate. Maybe, like Rockford, the hero sensed the trouble he was in. Maybe he didn't. Either way, it was time for a change. Not a big change. Nothing permanent. Maybe he'd dodge a few old friends for a while, maybe try out a few different bars. Something on a par with renting a condo in Vegas for six months before packing up and moving there.

What did the hero do?

What new resources or problem-solving style did the hero call upon to take his next step and navigate his way around whatever obstacle the villain dropped in his path? What does your brain-sleuthing tell you about the hero's new approach? More than likely he was inspired by something he'd done or thought about doing. Like the brusque hero who takes a stab at kindness or the timid hero who gets angry enough to speak his mind, although somewhat apologetically and certainly not at the top of his lungs. Or maybe he was more inspired by the loudmouth who decides to play it close to the vest and only squeal about his plans to half his usual audience.

The hero was ready to make a change, but not so ready that he was willing to burn all the bridges behind him. He made sure the six-month deposit on the condo was refundable.

HERO TRIES SOMETHING DIFFERENT

THE HERO COULD DO THIS

OR SOMETHING A LITTLE DIFFERENT

OR SOMETHING NOT TOO DIFFERENT BUT WHOLLY UNTHOUGHT OF

What's your choice for what the hero did?

You don't have to consult your story detective manual to find out what's next. By now you know the drill.

FIELD REPORT WORKSHEET

PEOPLE	PLACES	EVENTS WORTH NOTING

WITNESS REPORT

WITNESS	WHAT HAPPENED	WHERE	WHEN	QUOTES

Rockford tries to clear his schedule so he can spend time fishing. You, on the other hand, clear your schedule so you can have more time to add a short paragraph to your final report.

FINAL REPORT ENTRY 6

Chances are, the hero's move didn't deter the villain from his path. Maybe he wasn't enthralled by the hero's attempt to break with his past. Maybe he didn't care. All that was on the villain's mind was keeping after what he wanted, upping the ante for the hero along the way.

What does your brain-sleuthing point you toward? The villain wasn't making it any easier for the hero. What was the villain's next move?

VILLAIN UPS THE ANTE

THE VILLAIN COULD UP THE ANTE THIS WAY

OR MAYBE EVEN THIS WAY

OR HE COULD PULL SOMETHING OUT OF LEFT FIELD

How far up did the villain push things? Exactly how did things go down?

FIELD REPORT WORKSHEET

PEOPLE	PLACES	EVENTS WORTH NOTING

WITNESS REPORT

WITNESS	WHAT HAPPENED	WHERE	WHEN	QUOTES

You found that old thrust-and-parry still alive, and not just between the hero and the villain. It's was also there between the hero and his past. Before going any further, though, you decide it's time for dinner. The good news is, nobody will have a .45 in your ribs. The bad news is, while you eat, you need to catch up on paperwork and add what you've learned to your final report.

When you write up your notes, give the villain's move a decent paragraph.

FINAL REPORT ENTRY 7

Turns out the day wasn't such a waste of time after all. In fact, it turned out pretty well. Up until now, the hero's been routinely deflecting the villain's moves like Rockford routinely waits for a case to find him. Now you've seen the hero change. Rockford's always going to be Rockford. He'll always ask his friends—who are just this side of legal—for help. He'll always cross paths with clients who can't open up a box of cereal without finding a gangster as the prize inside.

But the hero's a different story. He has a real chance at breaking away.

EXAMPLE

Until now, Francine has been driven by the need to become famous not only to make her mark, but to rescue Stanley from his boring ancestry. She's driven enough to turn to bank robbery to keep her dream—or obsession—alive. But now, Horace's art has given Francine the cushion she needs to keep writing.

If life continues this way for Francine, there's no reason for her to change and the story sputters out. What we have to deduce as story detectives is what changed and how that changed Francine. The two major events are (1) Francine has money again, and (2) Horace is getting noticed, and he's enjoying it. Let's upset something, make things worse. Ignoring for a moment *why* it could happen, let's brain-sleuth *what* could happen.

HERO TRIES SOMETHING DIFFERENT

THE HERO COULD DO THIS

Decides she's no writer and gives up.

Doesn't want to depend on Horace, so she robs another bank, and this time makes sure she gets away with the money.

OR SOMETHING A LITTLE DIFFERENT

Decides she's not a writer and switches to a new form of expression, maybe one that directly conflicts with Horace.

OR SOMETHING NOT TOO DIFFERENT BUT WHOLLY UNTHOUGHT OF

Decides to help Horace with his art.

We can cast aside the first and third ideas. Choose the first, and the story is over. Choose the third, and Francine hasn't changed; she's the same person, just in different work clothes. One idea on the list, though, shows some potential. What if Francine decides to help Horace? Until now, everything Francine's done has been to make herself famous. But this is different. Now she wants to make Horace famous.

How might she help? She could be his assistant, but then the story would shift to being about Horace and his art. That's always been a possibility. We considered it early on, when we chose Francine as the hero, but let's see if we can stick with her for now. A good story detective always looks for the worst possible situation for the hero, so what if Francine's help resulted in Horace becoming more famous and Francine becoming less famous? That would put Francine in an absolutely awful position.

What if Horace is still making art, but now there's no money in it? The sales were a fad stimulated by Francine's antics in the bank. As that story faded from the public's mind, so did Horace's art sales. Francine's fortunes would have changed slightly. Yes, she's out of money again, but she has gained a resource. She has a husband whose work is in demand under the right circumstances—namely, if there are news stories about naked women and exploding cans of vegetables.

We don't have to brain-sleuth Francine's next step. She's going to rob another bank. What's different, though, is that Francine is about to help somebody else achieve the fame she's striving for. Yes, Horace's fame appears to help Francine, but the collision path in this story involves two people on separate paths to fame, and it's not clear whether they both can have it.

FINAL REPORT ENTRY 6

As the incident in the bank fades from view, so does Horace's art sales. The gallery stops calling. Likewise, the reporters. Francine does the only thing she can think of. She puts on another disguise, her fur coat, and nothing else, and explodes another can of vegetables in another bank. Creamed spinach this time. Although she demands cash to cover up, she makes no attempt to take the money. In no time, Horace's art is back in high demand.

Horace is famous again. He's going to do something to exploit that fame, and whatever it is, it will have a negative effect on Francine. That's what villains do. They get in the way of heroes.

VILLAIN UPS THE ANTE

THE VILLAIN COULD UP THE ANTE THIS WAY

Accepts invitations to parties.

Hires a publicist.

OR MAYBE EVEN THIS WAY

Begins eying other women.

Adopts an affected air of aloofness.

OR HE COULD PULL SOMETHING OUT OF LEFT FIELD

Ignores Francine.

Francine is hardly the kind of person who would enjoy, or tolerate, being snubbed, so any of these moves by Horace—which he would do not to hurt Francine but to enjoy what he sees as some well-deserved validation of his art—would up the pressure, the ante, for Francine.

What if we combine some of these ideas? Horace goes to these parties and is captivated by another woman—that would be worse than Horace simply going to the parties for their own sake. What if the woman he's captivated by is the mystery woman who's been setting off creamed corn and spinach in the banks? What if he talks about her as an artist, a kindred spirit?

FINAL REPORT ENTRY 7

Francine feels she is losing her husband. In between working around the clock on his art, Horace travels to New York to make the round of celebrity parties where he seems to pay attention to everyone but her. At one soirée, he is fawned over by all manner of celebrities, including Arnold, the pig from <u>Green Acres</u>.

Horace also announces that the person he'd most like to meet is the mystery woman who explodes the cans of vegetables in banks. He calls her a kindred spirit, and says that her performance art is making a wonderful statement. To Francine, that is akin to her husband running off with another woman.

The story has taken a few twists as the cause-and-effect chain lengthens. What's important, though, is the way Francine's plight has worsened. This is a key ingredient of any good story. Cause and effect, or action and reaction, aside, from the hero's perspective things always go downhill. The question is, how far down do they go?

Chapter 15

The Case of the
Bold Bravado

The hero's dossier that's sitting on your desk has every i and t in the hero's life dotted and crossed. Some maybe twice. Thing is, the hero is changing and pretty soon might leave that old dossier behind. Now more than ever, you've got to think like the hero. You've got to get inside your "new" hero's head. You know you can do it—after all, getting into a hero's head is how you earned your chops.

Of course, it couldn't hurt to get a second opinion. When it comes to getting into a suspect's head, you've got two people you can ask for help, and according to the papers, Freud is dead.

Best to call in New York City's finest, Detective Robert Goren—Bobby to his friends.

Give Detective Goren (is anybody really his friend?) a lock of hair, a list of credit card charges, or a suspect's favorite song, and he will open that ever-present portfolio of his and write a dossier on the suspect faster than your girlfriend changes her mind about you. In his spare time, he'll predict the suspect's next three moves like an IBM computer playing chess against Garry Kasparov.

"Your hero self-destructed," he says, offering his help before you can say a word. Goren not only knows his own moves, he knows yours. "It's all in here," he says, thumbing through the dossier you prepared and pulling it out from under your nose when you try to see where he's pointing.

"This hero committed to his cause, felt good about it, got set up by the villain, and wound up in deep despair."

"I thought the case was pretty routine, but …."

"I'm right, aren't I? I can see it. That little muscle right here." He points to a spot between his eyebrows. "I'm right, and there's something you want to say." You notice Goren doesn't apologize for the interruption.

The trouble is, there *is* something you want to say. This back-and-forth game is remarkably similar to one Goren played with Nicole Wallace when she set him up to hound a suspect to death. Literally. Is Goren describing the hero's experience, or his own?

"She set me up, you know. Nicole Wallace. That's what's bothering you. Am I setting you up?" Goren half-smiles. "That's good. You don't take things at *face* value. *Face value.* That's a little joke. It's your face that gives you away. Right here." He pokes you between the eyes.

"I guess I can take it from here," you say, but Goren shows no signs of leaving. He's got his head next to yours, cocked a bit to one side.

"You're feeling confident. Just like the hero." You start to issue a denial, but Goren's not listening. He's thumbing through your dossier. Then he scribbles something in his portfolio and pulls out the page. "This is where your hero went," he says, but he won't let you see the paper. He dangles it just out of your reach, as if it's a carrot on a stick. "Not yet. What do you think the hero did? How did he commit to his cause? If you were the villain, what would you have done to set up the hero?"

He holds up the sheet of paper, but this time your hand is quicker than his eye. You snatch it away. It's blank on both sides.

"Gotcha," Goren says as he backs out of your office. At least he doesn't slam the door.

Maybe Goren's right. Or maybe he was playing with you. But you're thinking that if Goren could be a victim of overconfidence, it could happen to the hero—or to you.

Best to take some time and revisit the hero's baggage and go through his resources. What has he added? New skills? New information? New friends or contacts? Did a long-lost relative leave him a surprise windfall? Money? Stocks? A haunted house? The state of Iowa? Did his confidence level change? Up or down? Why? If he got new information, what was it? A few shreds of information that didn't make sense? Or did he learn enough to impersonate a Wall Street banker or an airline pilot?

His new attitude is important, too. Besides his confidence, all sorts of other parts of his personality could have shifted. Perhaps his curiosity, assertiveness, determination, ambivalence, forcefulness, or judgment made a U-turn right in the middle of Main Street. What about the baggage the hero was ready to unload? Friends? Fear? Hesitation? Doubt? His whole identity?

Pull out the hero's dossier, see what's there—and what's not—and update it to reflect the changes.

UPDATE HERO'S DOSSIER

WHAT'S CHANGED	HOW CHANGED	WHY CHANGED

The day looks a little brighter as it dawns on you that your brain-sleuthing just got a bit easier. The old hero might have been holding back, but the new hero was ready to go all the way. That's what Goren was talking about when he said the hero committed. The hero was like Rockford, with one gumshoe planted firmly in his old life, but he took a step that meant he couldn't pretend nothing happened.

It's the old story of the honest-to-a-fault hero committing a crime or the spy selling secrets to the enemy, but the hero doesn't have to make an illegal move. Heroes have walked out of their lives by quitting their jobs in a huff, selling their belongings, moving to a new state or a new country, or giving their money away to charity. It's not something you would do, but you're not running through a story while running away from the villain, so who's to say?

Whatever the hero did, he's not on a leave of absence from his old life—he's AWOL. There are no timeouts or do-overs. Now, do some brain-sleuthing and figure out what the hero did and why there's no turning back.

THE HERO COMMITS

THE HERO COULD DO SOMETHING LIKE THIS

OR EVEN DO SOMETHING LIKE THIS

OR THE HERO COULD SURPRISE EVEN HERSELF BY DOING SOME-THING LIKE THIS

What did the hero—the new hero—do, once he decided to go for it? Of course, be sure to report on how he did it.

FIELD REPORT WORKSHEET

PEOPLE	PLACES	EVENTS WORTH NOTING

WITNESS REPORT

WITNESS	WHAT HAPPENED	WHERE	WHEN	QUOTES

FINAL REPORT ENTRY 8

So much excitement and it's not even lunchtime. It's been an impressive morning. You've seen the hero throw all his eggs into one basket while you've used up just about every metaphor you have for the hero committing to solving his problem. Now it's going to get rough for both you. For the hero, there's no turning back. For you, there are no more gumshoe slang expressions.

It's also been an impressive morning because of the way Detective Goren called the shots about what happened. But Goren also said that when the hero went all in, he also left himself open for the villain to set him up. Goren didn't elaborate, but you've been around this block before. The hero felt confident and even cocky. He was thinking he was in control. Problem is, he was more like a kid whose old man just took the training wheels off his bicycle. He had the speed. He had the momentum. What he didn't have was experience. He didn't know he was out of control. All the villain had to do was aim the hero into a dead-end alley where the wall at the back was one unforgiving foe.

What did the villain plan for the unsuspecting hero? It doesn't make a difference if the villain and the hero are one and the same. The part of the hero that's out to stop him from solving his problem can be just as determined as a Nicole Wallace. And worse, that villain is working from the inside, with more access to the hero than Nicole ever had to Goren. If you were the villain, what would you have done?

THE VILLAIN SETS UP THE HERO

THE VILLAIN COULD DO SOMETHING DEVIOUS LIKE THIS

OR HE COULD DO SOMETHING EVEN MORE DEVIOUS LIKE THIS

OR THE VILLAIN COULD OUT-DEVIOUS HIMSELF BY DOING SOMETHING LIKE THIS

What did the villain have in store for the hero? Would it have made Nicole Wallace proud, or made her look like an amateur villain?

You have to feel sorry for the hero as he walked into the darkest moment of this story. You have to admire the villain for the way he made the hero's situation worse. Most of all, you have to do your field work and commit the details to paper.

FIELD REPORT WORKSHEET

PEOPLE	PLACES	EVENTS WORTH NOTING

WITNESS REPORT

WITNESS	WHAT HAPPENED	WHERE	WHEN	QUOTES

FINAL REPORT ENTRY 9

Goren knew the hero was headed for a fall. Now the hero knows it, too. He fell for the setup and made a bold move. How bad was it? What does your brain-sleuthing reveal about what the hero did? What did it cost him in resources and ego? The hero was counting on those resources— friends, allies, and assets—to be there to help him out on the other side. Unfortunately, what he did cost him part of what he was counting on. What resources did he lose? What skills became worthless? What knowledge became suspicious? What assets did he put out of reach?

ALL IS LOST

WHAT DID HERO DO	RESOURCES LOST	WHY LOST

What move did the hero make? In the end, what move cost him the most resources and snatched success from under his nose, the way Goren snatched the dossier from under yours?

How did the hero's choice play out in the field?

FIELD REPORT WORKSHEET

PEOPLE	PLACES	EVENTS WORTH NOTING

WITNESS REPORT

WITNESS	WHAT HAPPENED	WHERE	WHEN	QUOTES

All that's left is writing a short paragraph in your final report to complete your descriptions of what the hero and villain did.

FINAL REPORT ENTRY 10

Now the day is over. Before leaving the office, you look in the mirror and tell yourself that the case is practically solved. From somewhere in the glass, Goren's finger reaches out and pokes you between the eyes.

EXAMPLE

Francine is famous, only her fame isn't based on what she'd hoped. She's famous for being the mysterious muse of her husband. Worse (and we story detectives love that word), she's afraid she's no longer the love of his life. Before considering Francine's next move, let's see how her resources have changed.

UPDATE HERO'S DOSSIER

WHAT'S CHANGED	HOW CHANGED	WHY CHANGED
Taste of fame	She's somewhat famous	Horace has inadvertently made her so
Fame	She's anonymous	She could go to jail if she's found out
Horace	She fears she's losing him	He seems aloof, drunk with celebrity, captivated by his mystery woman
Finances	In good shape	As long as she blows up canned vegetables, Horace sells art

Francine must choose what to do next.

THE HERO COMMITS

THE HERO COULD DO SOMETHING LIKE THIS

Blow up more cans of vegetables.

Confide in Carla.

Throw herself back into finishing her book.

OR EVEN DO SOMETHING LIKE THIS

Confess to Horace who she is to quash her jealousy.

OR THE HERO COULD SURPRISE EVEN HERSELF BY DOING SOMETHING LIKE THIS

Abandon her book and be the unsung hero behind Horace's art.

Except for confiding in Carla, which doesn't seem to settle anything, all the ideas on the list show promise. At times like these, it's usually effective to ask which choice makes the situation worse, creates the most conflict, or both.

Continuing to help Horace behind the scenes seems to smooth the way for both of them. There doesn't seem to be much conflict or disaster there. Maybe Francine could get caught, but Francine in jail takes her out of the game, and therefore the story. Suddenly, she must find a way to escape the criminal justice system. That could be a great story, but it's not *this* story. After embarrassing Stanley, Francine needs fame to redeem herself in Stanley's eyes and her own. What action can Francine take to make that redemption less possible?

This is a tough call. There are strong arguments for Francine quashing her jealousy and continuing on behind the scenes. However, confessing to Horace that she's his muse is a step forward, and forward steps usually make the most sense.

In good story detective style, we should ask how and where the confession happens to maximize conflict. All else being equal, let's pick a location with an emotional punch. In public? At home? Bedrooms carry more than their share of emotional baggage. For maximum conflict, it's hard to beat lovemaking, especially in a relationship that's had its share of recent rocky moments.

We'll have to skip the field report on this one. Unless Horace and Francine have some peculiar neighbors, or the flies on their walls can speak, there aren't going to be any witnesses.

FINAL REPORT ENTRY 8

After a few more bank "performances," Francine can't take it any longer. She hates how Horace fawns over her alter ego. She hates even more that he seems so romantically disengaged from her. One evening, just before bed, she comes out of the bathroom dressed in her fur coat and nothing else, snuggles up to him, and asks how he'd like to make some real explosions with his mystery muse.

Horace is about to set up Francine for a fall. He's not going to do it intentionally; he's not a mean-spirited man. And Horace does love Francine. What are his options?

THE VILLAIN SETS UP THE HERO

THE VILLAIN COULD DO SOMETHING DEVIOUS LIKE THIS

He is happy to find out the truth.

He doesn't believe her and wants proof.

He wants to know what's behind this strange behavior (the confession, not the bank business).

OR HE COULD DO SOMETHING EVEN MORE DEVIOUS LIKE THIS

He has sex with her, and they rekindle their romance.

He wants to talk about new art projects they can do together.

OR THE VILLAIN COULD OUT-DEVIOUS HIMSELF BY DOING SOMETHING LIKE THIS

He spurns her advances as fantasy and turns on the television or rolls over and goes to sleep.

We can rule out Horace being delighted to know the truth because it drains the story of any tension and conflict. Turning things around, if Horace doesn't buy Francine's confession, that certainly retains the conflict. How should Horace dismiss her?

Often, conflict results when two people see the same situation in different ways. To Francine, the lovemaking may be her way of getting Horace to recognize that the woman he's infatuated with is the woman at his side. To Horace, the lovemaking may be Francine's attempt to unselfishly feed his sexual fantasy of making love to his mystery muse. If that isn't conflict, nothing is.

FINAL REPORT ENTRY 9

Francine and Horace make passionate love. In the afterglow, Francine anticipates cuddling close to her wonderful husband, after confessing to him about her double life. Horace misses the confession part completely, assuming Francine is helping him live out his fantasy of sex with his muse. Saying they "have words" doesn't do justice to the situation, which is best summed up by Horace's sleeping on the living room couch.

Although Horace's actions weren't meant to upset Francine, they set her up to make a desperate move. Instead of her confession to Horace earning her the recognition she was after, it earned her ridicule (at least in her mind). She needs to take an even bolder step. She's ready for it. What are her options?

ALL IS LOST

WHAT DID HERO DO	RESOURCES LOST	WHY LOST
Confess to police	Freedom, money for lawyer	She'll be in jail
Rob bank and take big money	Freedom if caught, friends and family if on the run	In jail
Rob bank out of disguise	Freedom, money for lawyer	Police will be hunting her down
Go on talk show and confess	Support of family and friends	She'd be just another kook

If the police confirm she's been blowing up canned vegetables in banks, the world will have to believe her—certainly Horace will. There's a steep price tag attached, however, and jail is just the beginning. She could lose the support of her friends and family. Even a modest sentence will rob her of her prime senior citizen years. Legal fees will quickly drain their savings. Horace's art may fall out of favor again. But confessing to the police would solidify her fame and win back Horace's attention. It would seem we've uncovered Francine's next move.

We haven't yet asked ourselves if getting thrown in jail is the worst that could happen. Maybe the worst that could happen is that the police don't believe her. They think she's one of those fame seekers or, worse, a kook. So does Horace, Joan, and everyone else. Far from being famous, Francine is even more insignificant than before.

Imagine we compiled our field report in the police station by interviewing some detectives. Maybe there were a couple of suspects in the room who were waiting to be interviewed for other offenses. For fun, one of those suspects could be a prostitute. They would describe

Francine's confession. From their statements, we could compile the next part of our final report.

FINAL REPORT ENTRY 10

The next morning, Francine marches into the middle of the busy squad room and in a loud voice, confesses to being the mystery bank robber. When the detectives on duty hardly notice, Francine opens her coat and stands there naked. After a careful discussion among the police, who rely on the expert opinion of a couple prostitutes on their way to the courthouse, all present conclude it isn't her. The real mystery woman is considerably younger, with rounder breasts and a firmer tummy. Francine is held in custody, for her own protection, until Horace can take her home.

In the aftermath, Horace fears Francine is having a breakdown. Joan is furious Francine would lie just to make herself look important to Stanley. And when Stanley finds out Horace has met Arnold the pig, he invites Horace, not Francine, to speak at career day. Joan insists Horace come without the pig ... and without Francine.

Francine's life has bottomed out. Her resource collection has been bled nearly dry. Any remaining resources seem useless. Francine must face failure, failure—and this is an important point to remember—forged by her own hand.

Chapter 16

The Case of the Other Hand

The alarm came down like a hammer this morning, reminding you there are days in every case when no "remuneration commensurate with results" is worth getting out of bed for. It started last night. Those "certain friends and acquaintances" got wind that the hero really stepped in it. Apparently having lost enough confidence in you to fill Lake Huron, they're holding you responsible for not finding the hero in time and have decided you need their help.

Half of them believe it's up to you to pull the hero out of this mess. Half believe the hero is due for a stroke of incredible luck, like finding the key to his jail cell tucked under the mattress or inheriting the money he needs from a recently deceased third cousin twice removed on his father's side who, incredibly, has no other living relatives. The third half figures it's all over for the hero and is busy dividing up his estate.

If you're lucky, you can pretend you're opening the door to pick up the newspaper and sneak out while they're squabbling. You know that what-ever happened, the hero's fate is in his own hands. He may have gotten help from friends, allies, or Lady Luck, but even that old dame wasn't going to hang around to do all the heavy lifting.

His resources are gone. His friends, old contacts, new contacts, hidden treasures, hoarded items, and assets are all useless to him now. His repu-tation is shattered. Speaking the truth is of no value if no one's bothering to listen. More than luck, the hero could use a little help from Quincy.

Not that the hero could get Quincy's help, even if he tried. Quincy's a soft touch all right, especially for a coroner. And it's not that he's difficult to talk to. For a guy who spends his time around corpses, Quincy's remarkably social. It's just that once he's on a case, Quincy likes to have the last word … and the first word … and all the words in between.

Maybe because in his cases the people he's closest to don't talk back, Quincy isn't inclined to let go of his stream of logic any more than a bulldog is inclined to let go of a mailman's leg. Quincy is also extremely disciplined and logical when it comes to stringing together clues. Once he used logic, intuition, and common sense—and enough who, what, when, where, why, and how questions to fill Lake Superior—to reconstruct the image of a murder victim from a single bone.

That resourcefulness is what the hero needed.

You know what resources the hero lost. What does he have left? What new resources did the hero add since you last updated his dossier? What new scraps of information, insignificant details, and casual contacts belong in there now? What did he gain that hardly seemed important at the time? Did a street kid show him how to pick a lock? Did an unfortunate encounter with a lawyer leave him with some unanticipated knowledge about contracts? Did an unattended hospital computer screen give him a glimpse at a relative's condition? Did a picture in a wet newspaper he kicked into the gutter turn out to be a critical clue? Did the hero have a second chance to correct a previous failure? Had he learned enough to succeed this time? That opportunity might have been the resource he was looking for.

Maybe luck did play a role in solving the hero's problem. Maybe the hero did find the key to his problem tucked under the mattress. Did he recognize it? Did he know what to do with it? Did he learn enough to help himself?

Like Quincy, the hero was handed a single bone with which to reconstruct his success. Find that bone.

This could be the hardest brain-sleuthing so far, and you're standing outside your door in your bathrobe, hoping you remembered to bring the front-door key.

HERO'S NEW RESOURCES (FINDING THE BONE)

PEOPLE	MONEY	NEW ASSETS	NEW PLACES
EXPERIENCES	**SKILLS**	**KNOWLEDGE**	**INTERESTS**

From where he is and what he's got to work with, the hero, like Quincy, pieced together the whole picture. Quincy found the killer. The hero found a way out.

HERO'S WAY OUT

THIS MIGHT WORK

OR SOMETHING UNUSUAL LIKE THIS MIGHT WORK

OR MAYBE SOMETHING EVEN MORE UNEXPECTED MIGHT WORK

What did the hero do? How did he solve the puzzle? What did he piece together to turn certain hopelessness into hope?

When Quincy cracked his case, he celebrated by using himself as bait to catch a killer. You, on the other hand, get to celebrate your case by uncovering the details. The end of the case is closer than you could have imagined the first day those "certain friends and acquaintances" came calling.

FIELD REPORT WORKSHEET

PEOPLE	PLACES	EVENTS WORTH NOTING

WITNESS REPORT

WITNESS	WHAT HAPPENED	WHERE	WHEN	QUOTES

For the first time in a long time, you can see the hero turning full tilt toward not just solving his problem, but also doing just what those "certain friends and acquaintances" seem to fear most—returning to his life a changed person. Not surprisingly, they're clamoring for details. Where's the hero? What happened? Where did he go?

You're tempted to call a confab so you can bask in the glory as you reveal to everyone the details of how you stalked this story, but now is not the time. The hero still has something to prove—something from way back in your notes.

For now, you'll just add another paragraph about the hero's comeback to your final report. Until you have everything nailed down, and with "remuneration commensurate with results" emphasizing results, there's no need to rush—not until you've boned up on the details.

FINAL REPORT ENTRY 11

EXAMPLE

At this point, Francine seems shut out from her dream. She's famous among only her family and friends. Her fame—if that's what we want to call it—comes from her being on the verge of a breakdown. Worse (there's that word again), she's been forbidden to see Stanley. The resources she started this story with are either gone or ineffective. Let's see what new resources she's picked up or otherwise has to work with.

HERO'S NEW RESOURCES (FINDING THE BONE)

PEOPLE	MONEY	NEW ASSETS	NEW PLACES
Horace is now focused on her	Her fortunes have gone up and down, but for now, money is not a problem		Police station, banks
EXPERIENCES	**SKILLS**	**KNOWLEDGE**	**INTERESTS**
How to hold a crowd's attention	Exploding canned vegetables	Confession helps even if it doesn't go as planned	Helping another be successful

Again here's an example that reminds us that not every column in every worksheet will have an entry. There doesn't seem to be a new asset for Francine to work with. If you can't think of an entry in a particular column, it's fine to move along to the ones that prove more fruitful.

Francine's in a bind. Without support from her friends and family, she has to depend on herself.

HERO'S WAY OUT

THIS MIGHT WORK

Return to her book.

Win back Stanley's respect.

Pursue a different route to fame.

OR SOMETHING UNUSUAL LIKE THIS MIGHT WORK

OR MAYBE SOMETHING EVEN MORE UNEXPECTED MIGHT WORK

This time, Francine's situation presents us with a major challenge. After all, if Francine has lost just about everything, she isn't going to have much to work with. We can start by focusing on what she wants the most. The stronger the hero's desire, the harder the hero will fight for it. All along, Francine's goal has been to make her mark and give Stanley the cachet that comes from having a famous relative. Fame may be out of reach, but she still owes Stanley some sort of explanation or resolution.

One of her new resources is how she felt after she confessed she was the mystery bank robber. Although things didn't go as planned, her confession did lift the burden of living a double life off her shoulders. Still headstrong, Francine could go, on her own, to Stanley's career fair, where she'll confess she's messed things up.

As story detectives, we know things can't be that easy for her.

What happens when Francine gets there? Looking over her new list of resources, one seems interesting. Francine has learned how to help others. Remember, the whole mystery bank robber affair began when she discovered that her blowing up canned vegetables helped sell Horace's art. Helping others was not a trait she brought into this story—it's an indication that she's changed. Let's use that when Francine travels to Stanley's school to make things right between them.

Francine could help three people: Horace, Joan, or Stanley. Francine is focused on Stanley, so let's see how Francine could help him. We know he's been picked on because he's boring and comes from a boring family. Francine might help him become less boring. How? There doesn't seem to be an answer yet, so let's get Francine to career day.

She's not supposed to be there, so we have her sneak into Stanley's school. She doesn't want to roam the halls, so she ducks into a classroom. If the room is empty, that doesn't help us, so let's put some people in there. Francine walks into a classroom where students and parents are preparing refreshments. What refreshments? Cookies. Cupcakes. Brownies. Lemonade. That sounds like kids' stuff.

This is one of those moments when ideas just present themselves for no apparent reason. Of course, we've paved the way by asking who, what, when, where, why, and how questions throughout our story detective career, but when an idea just pops up, it still feels like magic. What if the lemonade being served is just awful? What if Francine is a lemonade connoisseur? She shows the parents and kids how to make some from her special recipe. What if she tells everyone she got that recipe from Stanley?

Will it work? There's only one way to find out, and that's to go with it and see where it leads. The idea seems to have the qualities we've been looking for. Instead of putting the focus on her, Francine helps Stanley and, in doing so, rescues him from obscurity. There's only one problem: Francine is not a lemonade connoisseur. There's nothing in her dossier about lemonade, and she's learned nothing about lemonade in the story so far. You probably know from experience how disappointing a story becomes when the resolution depends on a twist that comes out of nowhere.

This is why we need to be flexible.

We need to go back earlier in the story and give Francine the expertise she needs to allow her to find her way out through lemonade. In writer parlance, this is called "laying it in." We don't want to draw too much attention to Francine's lemonade expertise lest we create a situation in which the audience is distracted, wondering why we've made a big deal out of something so seemingly unimportant. We just need a passing mention early on in our final report.

Here's one possible fix, a modification to final report entry 2:

> Back home the next day, and despite her doctor's orders, Francine goes for her usual morning run. Not only does she double-time it, she makes a point of telling virtually everyone she passes—nearly a dozen startled runners and twice as many passers-by—that she is in the best shape ever.
>
> For the next few weeks, Francine seems to shut herself off from the rest of the world. She works longer and longer hours. *She no longer meets Horace at the door with a glass of her special lemonade when he returns from blowing up canned vegetables in the woods near their home.* Horace jokes that he doesn't have a wife and begins calling Francine his "boarder." Oblivious, Francine cranks out page after page of her book as if racing some competing, imaginary author toward an equally imaginary finish line.

We can add material to our outline from interviews with the parents and students in the room. Francine still has some of her old qualities; according to the witnesses, she took the parents and some of the students to task, declaring she wouldn't serve the lemonade to her beloved husband if he were dying of thirst.

FINAL REPORT ENTRY 11

Francine secretly travels to visit Stanley at career day, intent on confessing that she tried to make him proud, pretending not to be insignificant. It's just that they come from a long line of insignificant people. Not wanting to be caught and create a scene, Francine sneaks into the school and ducks into a classroom, only to find it is being used by parents and students to prepare cookies and lemonade for the event. It is the worst lemonade she has ever tasted. Proclaiming she would never let her husband drink that awful stuff, she proceeds to show the kids how to make lemonade properly. It is a huge hit, and Francine credits the recipe to her brilliant nephew, Stanley.

Francine did find a way out, and the route led through her backstory. Of course, we had to add an asset (lemonade expertise) to her backstory first, but the paths writers follow often make unexpected leaps through time and space.

Part 3

The Conclusion

Chapter 17

The Case of the Caper Cleanup

You sense your work is almost done. In fact, you're hoping today is the day you get out in front of your hero. What you should hope is that you can be a little more like Adrian Monk.

Maybe you think you are like Monk. You see yourself as the solver of impossible stories. Maybe you're eccentric, demanding, unpredictable, and logically illogical, just like Monk. You're Monk with all the neuroses left out.

Except there's one neurotic behavior you need to keep.

Mixed in with Monk's concerns about shaking hands, nudity, lack of symmetry, loud noises, soft noises, dirt, dust, germs, airborne particles, weather reports, and pencils of unequal lengths is a deep distrust of loose ends. Not the kind that will cause your shirt to unravel, although those belong on the list, too.

Monk would never sleep if he knew his case wasn't sewn up tight—and finished off with a proper knot. If Monk were on this case, he wouldn't be sleeping very well—all the more reason for you to be wide awake, too, especially if you don't know what you're looking for.

Somewhere in the story, someone put events in motion that took on a life of their own. You've got one last job to do. Figure out what those events were and what the hero did about it. Because if the hero left an end dangling, this story may not have a happy ending.

Monk would have no trouble finding out. He'd simply obsess over the problem, day and night, until he drove everyone around him crazy. At some point, the suspect in the case would probably confess merely to enjoy the peace and quiet of state prison. Chances are, people who weren't suspects would confess just to get Monk to go back where he came from.

What's left over in the case? Did the hero put some plan in motion earlier on? Did he start a project and then put it aside or decide not to finish it? Did he ask friends, allies, or contacts to do something for him and then forget to follow up in the crush of dealing with the villain? Once his world calmed down, the hero might have decided to quash the plan because it was no longer necessary. In fact, if it went the way he hoped, the plan would have served to get the hero into trouble so deep and wide, he might have regretted every step of this adventure.

If it's not the hero, then perhaps the loose end has the villain's finger-prints all over it. He may be defeated, but like a fish flopping around on the pier, being pulled out of the water doesn't mean all the fight has gone out of him. Even if he's totally out of the picture, the villain may have planted a metaphorical time bomb and then died, vanished, or clammed up tight before anyone knew where the bomb was or how to disarm it. Whatever the plan was, it could potentially blow up in the hero's face.

And just because the villain's out of the picture doesn't mean his spirit isn't living on in the hearts of his allies, who might be carrying on the battle, like soldiers lost in the jungle who have no idea the war is over. For the allies, it's all about loyalty or revenge. Don't count on them giving up without a fight.

Finally, for everything the hero's been through and everything he's learned, don't be surprised if there's one bit of information missing, one detail the hero needs to know, one experience he has to have, one group of skeptics he has to convince, one bouncer he has to sweet talk into let-ting him cross the velvet rope to enter the club of successful heroes.

Monk would go over the case, step by step, to be sure he didn't miss something. And so should you. If the loose end that stands in the hero's way isn't visible immediately, review your field notes, final report notes, and dossier for a clue. If necessary, turn to the scene of earlier events and re-interview witnesses or look for new ones. Talk to the hero's friends and allies, both old and new, and Monk-icize them to death with your questions. Either find what you're looking for or be sure it doesn't exist.

THE FINAL LOOSE END

THE LOOSE END COULD BE

OR IT MIGHT BE SOMEWHAT LESS OBVIOUS, LIKE

OR IT COULD BE SOMETHING YOU THOUGHT YOU'D NEVER THINK OF

What is it? What does your Monk-ian instinct tell you the hero had to take care of? Now that you know what the hero has to do, how did he do it? How did he tie off that loose end? What kind of knot did he use?

TYING UP THE LOOSE END

THE HERO COULD TIE IT ALL OFF BY

OR DO SOMETHING A BIT MORE UNCONVENTIONAL, SUCH AS

OR TIE THINGS UP WITH A NEEDLE PULLED OUT OF A HAYSTACK, SUCH AS

You know what he had to do. You know how he did it. You just need to fill in the details.

FIELD REPORT WORKSHEET

PEOPLE	PLACES	EVENTS WORTH NOTING

WITNESS REPORT

WITNESS	WHAT HAPPENED	WHERE	WHEN	QUOTES

That's it. The hero overcame his final obstacle—at least you hope so. You'll know for sure in a little while, but for now, channeling your inner Monk has served you well. Satisfy your obsessive nature with another paragraph describing what the hero did, and your case is all cleaned up. Then go wash your hands.

FINAL REPORT ENTRY 12

EXAMPLE

Let's see what loose ends might be floating around this story.

THE FINAL LOOSE END

THE LOOSE END COULD BE

Relationship with Horace.

Relationship with Stanley.

Relationship with Carla.

Relationship with Joan.

OR IT MIGHT BE SOMEWHAT LESS OBVIOUS, LIKE

Identity of the mystery bank robber.

OR IT COULD BE SOMETHING YOU THOUGHT YOU'D NEVER THINK OF

Possibility of Francine going to jail.

Out of these brain-sleuthing results, the possibility of whether she goes to jail is probably the one that poses the greatest threat to Francine. The police might still be looking for the mystery woman, and Francine may have left some clues behind that will ultimately lead to her downfall. With her life on a new, upward trajectory, perhaps we need to settle the question of whether Francine is on or off the hook for her exploits.

TYING UP THE LOOSE END

THE HERO COULD TIE IT ALL OFF BY

Getting arrested but charges are dropped.

Discovering the police have lost interest.

Discovering bank managers refuse to press charges because their business has gone up. (Banks are famous art sites now.)

OR DO SOMETHING A BIT MORE UNCONVENTIONAL, SUCH AS

Discovering police and press finally believe her, and becoming a pop art darling.

Persuading Horace to reveal the truth.

OR TIE THINGS UP WITH A NEEDLE PULLED OUT OF A HAY- STACK, SUCH AS

Someone else confesses.

Tying up a loose end is just that: bringing to a conclusion some thread in the story without taking the story off in another direction. We still need to answer the question of whether Francine achieves fame and sets things right with Stanley. That's something we want to reserve for the story's ending. Francine's arrest sounds as if it's beginning a new thread in which she has to prove her innocence. Her becoming a pop art darling feels more like it's a story ending rather than a loose end.

What we need is to conclude our story quickly and cleanly. As before, let's opt for something happening rather than nothing—as in nobody taking an action toward Francine. Let's try someone else confessing to the crime. Francine and Horace need to find out about the confession and, because we know Horace likes watching television in bed, we can recycle a familiar location. Familiar locations come in handy because their histories can work in our favor to set up expectations or conflict.

As before, we'll assume bedroom scenes don't come with witnesses to interview.

FINAL REPORT ENTRY 12

> *Back home and snuggling in bed, Horace and Francine watch an 11 o'clock news report of the police arresting a suspect who claims to be the mystery woman behind the explosions of canned vegetables in banks. The police are convinced the woman is the perpetrator because she has a history of unstable behavior. Francine laughs. Horace sighs. They both roll closer to each other, and Horace turns off the light.*

With the loose threads taken care of, it feels as if the story may have come to an end. Not yet. The story began, many chapters ago, with Francine wanting to make her mark. If she has, we haven't made the who, what, when, why and how of that clear. If she hasn't, well, we'll need to say something about that, instead.

Chapter 18

The Case of the Remaining Resolution

There comes a time in every detective's life when he knows whether he's in or out of the game. For Columbo, it's the look in his suspect's eye when he says, "Do you see what I'm saying, sir? How the only way you could have known that is if you were there when the murder took place?" For Banacek, it's the smile on his face and the cigar between his lips when he addresses a gathering of insurance executives. For House, it's when his eyes grow wide and he stares right through Wilson or Cuddy.

This is your moment.

Maybe you've known it from the day Peggy left your office. Maybe things have changed since then. Nevertheless, for the first time, you're leading the race. You're not the greyhound down at the track. You're the little mechanical rabbit, and everyone's chasing you.

You don't have to hail a cab today, because there's one waiting for you in front of the building. The usual morning traffic is nonexistent. You arrive at the site of the story's conclusion with plenty of time to claim a front-row seat. You're pretty sure you know what's going to happen, but heroes have a way of surprising even the craftiest story detectives, so you vow to stay put and fight the urge to introduce yourself to the hero, shake his hand, and grab a photo for your wall.

This is your moment, but it's the hero's day. Let things unwind in their own way.

You won't need to interview witnesses this time. You'll see it all firsthand—one paragraph, from your eyes to your final report. Those "certain friends and acquaintances" are about to get the answers they've been looking for.

FINAL REPORT ENTRY 13

EXAMPLE

In bringing a story to its conclusion, one of your objectives is finding a way to show the audience a resolution that ties up the story as quickly and as dramatically as possible. Delaying the inevitable leads only to frustration, anger, and often silliness. (Think of some of those early bad westerns in which the actor gets shot and spends three minutes stumbling across the screen before finally dying.)

We've always known Francine was going to make her mark and help out Stanley. We've always known Francine's face would be familiar, and that people would recognize her and her name. Now, we're there. We need to share our knowledge with the audience.

One twist in this story came when Francine gave Stanley credit for the lemonade recipe. Let's look there for inspiration for the ending, along with Francine's wish from way back that people would know her face and name. If we take things literally, people would recognize Francine's face when she walked down the street. They would recognize her name when someone introduced her to them. We could show those introductions literally, but introductions in films are tedious. It's better if we suggest Francine's fame by putting some thought into other representations of face and name.

FINAL REPORT ENTRY 13

Flash forward 20 years. At a small graveside ceremony, Francine's body is laid to rest alongside her dearly departed Horace. The officiating priest makes some comments about how in love and devoted they were to each other in their final years. Carla, in a wheelchair, sobs softly. Joan seeks support on Stanley's shoulder. Stanley has grown up to become a fine-looking man, and he is well dressed in an expensive black suit.

After the ceremony, Stanley and Joan climb into a limo and are whisked to the airport, where they board a private jet. As the plane speeds down the runway, the words "Aunt Fran's Fruit Drinks, Inc." on the side of the fuselage fly by. As the plane lifts off, the setting sun glints off the company's logo, a sketch of Francine's face, emblazoned on the plane's tail.

The moment's over. The hero's departed. Did it happen the way you expected or did circumstances surprise even you? Back at the office, you let the "certain friends and acquaintances" know you expect them in your office first thing tomorrow morning. You remind them to bring that "remuneration commensurate with results"—or at least as much of it as they can carry.

Chapter 19

The Case of the Inevitable Explanation

The story may be over, but your job isn't.

Today's the day you're going to give those "certain friends and acquaintances" what they've been bugging you for since the day they showed up with this case—and it's not the answer to what happened to the hero. After all, this isn't a game of chasing Waldo. Those "certain friends and acquaintances" aren't about to hand over all that "remuneration commensurate with results" for a postcard with "The butler did it" scribbled on one side and a color photo of the Statue of Liberty on the other. In return for digging you out from under those bills, those "certain friends and acquaintances" expect more than simple answers—they expect entertainment.

Any story detective worth his license can describe where the hero wound up. The big scores go to the detectives who turn their summations into shows that would make Barnum divorce Bailey and partner up with them instead.

How does your final report stack up? If you were to read it aloud, would those "certain friends and acquaintances" be fidgeting in their seats and putting away their wallets? Take a tip from Jessica Fletcher. She didn't just point a finger when she revealed the identity of the perpetrator, she wove a story—and she began her story by setting the scene.

"If you remember," she may say, "it was a dark and stormy night." With all that "remuneration commensurate with results" on the line, take some time to return to the beginning of your final report. That's right, the beginning.

Does your report kick off with an image? Something visual that gives those "certain friends and acquaintances" an idea of the story you're about to tell? Are they in for a mystery? A thriller? A comedy? Something out of this world? What kind of image belongs at the beginning of your report to set the scene for what follows?

SETTING THE SCENE

I COULD START THE STORY WITH AN IMAGE, LIKE

OR SOMETHING MORE UNUSUAL, LIKE

OR SOMETHING UNEXPECTED BUT QUITE EFFECTIVE, LIKE

Which image on your list can you imagine Mrs. Fletcher describing to the group gathered in front of her? Describe the image in as few of your best Mrs. Fletcher sentences as possible.

FINAL REPORT ENTRY 0

EXAMPLE

A good opening suggests the kind of story that follows. It never hurts if the opening sets up or alludes to some sort of dilemma for the hero.

SETTING THE SCENE

I COULD START THE STORY WITH AN IMAGE, LIKE

Francine captivates Stanley and his classmates.

Francine is strict and demanding.

Francine basks in the applause of a grateful class.

OR SOMETHING MORE UNUSUAL, LIKE

Francine is nervous talking to all those inquisitive faces.

Francine bores Stanley and his classmates.

OR SOMETHING UNEXPECTED BUT QUITE EFFECTIVE, LIKE

Francine walks out of the class when she can't get the students' attention.

We know Francine is headstrong, and that she needs to get her own way. She hardly seems like the kind of person to get along well with a group of elementary-school kids. At the same time, she wants recognition and fame, and that's where this story is heading, so she's not about to give up easily. Let's put all that in a paragraph that will begin our final report.

FINAL REPORT ENTRY 0

Under a banner that says "Career Day 1971," a prim, proper, and unimaginatively dressed Francine stands in front of her nephew Stanley's elementary school classmates. With all the enthusiasm she can muster—and for Francine, that's a formidable amount—she extols the virtues of working at the post office and the excitement of punching the first 3 digits of ZIP codes into a letter sorting machine for hours on end. Throughout the auditorium, kids fidget, talk, and use ballpoint pens to etch their initials into the wooden arms of their seats. As Francine continues, undaunted, we see Stanley sitting in the far corner of the auditorium, burying his face in his hands.

This opening accomplishes a host of objectives quickly and, most importantly, visually. It's 1971. Francine's style of dress lets us know she's far from an imaginative, creative individual. For whatever reason, she's a little out of touch with other people because her approach to making her job sound exciting is hardly working, yet she presses on. Francine is thoroughly humiliating and embarrassing Stanley, setting up a dilemma for Francine and alerting the audience to the direction the story will head.

You're ready to go. You know you've done your best. You stuck with it, through the highs and lows, and along the way you had the help of some of the greatest detectives in the business. In the end you did what story detectives have been doing since the beginning of time. You cracked the case. Why did you bother? Because that's what you do. You pile up bills. You worry about heroes and villains, about fresh meadows and dark alleys, about guns, knives, poisons, aliens, spaceships, errant meteors, and life after death.

Now you must do what story detectives have always done next. You must sit down those "certain friends and acquaintances," the ones who got you into this story in the first place, and tell them you were up to the task and that they're going to pay for everything they put you through.

Then, take a deep breath and tell them a story they'll never forget.

Epilogue

There's a certain exhilaration that comes from finishing your story. What began as little more than an impression—a setting, a character or two, an incident, a what-if idea—now has a tangible form and shape. You can read about it, see it in your mind, and envision it playing at the local Cineplex, watched by your "certain friends and acquaintances," all of whom gasp in unison when the words "Written by" appear on the screen right above your name.

Not to throw a medium popcorn and a drink on that dream, but there are a few more steps between what you have in your hands, or in your computer, and that Saturday night at the movies. In my classes, I find my students frequently ask the following questions after they've finished their story outlines and are anxious to proceed to their screenplays.

NOW I CAN WRITE MY SCREENPLAY, RIGHT?

Unlikely. There's no law against it, of course, but writing is a process of discovery. What you've discovered about your story is far more than what you knew about it before you began work on the outline that is your final report. There's still more to uncover before you know enough to comfortably write a full-length feature script.

WHAT'S A GOOD FIRST STEP?

The first step to take toward your feature script is rewriting your story outline. It's fair to say that, despite your best efforts, your story has some holes in it. More than likely, it contains jumps in the story logic that, if you hit them unexpectedly, will complicate your script-writing. You won't catch them all at the outline stage, but another pass over the story now will unearth the more obvious ones.

BUT I WON'T HAVE TO CHANGE TOO MUCH, RIGHT?

This can be a tough lesson to learn, and no book can teach it to you. It's one that comes from experience.

Learn to let go of what you've written. This outline isn't a script, and the script you develop from your outline isn't the final film. There will be parts of your outline that simply won't work in script form. Usually, these parts are the ones you feel are your greatest moments. You'll work with them, rewrite them, juggle them, curse at them, and beat yourself into believing you can't do without them.

No matter how much you love your script, and no matter how much the director loves your script, there will be scenes that work on the page but not on the screen. That riveting dialogue falls flat. That amazing scene in the alley isn't cinematic. The trick is to know when to stop inflicting mental anguish upon yourself and those around you. Only when you let go can you discover a new way of approaching the material.

IF I HAVE TO LET GO, WHAT HAPPENS TO ALL MY IDEAS?

The other side of letting go is knowing when to dig in. At many stages in your screenwriting career, you'll be asked to make changes to your outlines and scripts. Often, this won't be a request. The question is, when do you accede to the wishes of agents, producers, directors, actors, spouses, and the kid who delivers your pizza (if you're foolish enough to share a copy of your script with him even if he says his uncle is a producer)? This is always a judgment call, but over time, most writers find that as long as they stay true to the Simple Human Truths that brought them to their stories, they can stay flexible in the telling.

When it seems as if your Simple Human Truth is falling by the wayside and the new story is not one you want to tell, it may be time to politely seek other interested parties, or to put your story/script aside for a while. It just may be an idea whose time has not yet come.

WHAT AM I SUPPOSED TO DO WITH ALL THE MATERIAL I COMPILED IN MY DOSSIERS AND DIDN'T USE?

Hang on to it. You've still got a script to write. That's roughly 100 pages left to fill.

MY FRIENDS USE WORDS LIKE *PROTAGONIST, ANTAGONIST, SUBPLOT,* AND *FALSE ALLIES*—DON'T I HAVE TO KNOW THESE?

People often toss around words and phrases such as *act break, turning point, theme,* or *all-is-lost moment* because they've heard scripts should contain them. I've opted for more old-fashioned terminology—like *heroes* and *villains*—to help you focus on stalking your story without getting caught up in Hollywood name games.

That said, there are some terms you need to know. Here are a few of the important ones, and how these terms relate to the steps you've taken as a story detective:

Protagonist   This is the character this book refers to as the hero. The protagonist is who the story is about, and this term is more common than *hero* because the protagonist doesn't have to be good. He just has to be someone who moves the story forward through his actions and decisions.

Antagonist   This is the character the book refers to as the villain. Analogous to the protagonist, the antagonist doesn't have to be bad. The antagonist is simply the character whose plans conflict with the protagonist in such a way that both the protagonist and antagonist can't get what they want.

Moral   The script's Simple Human Truth.

Three-act structure   The traditional dramatic structure upon which writers build most films (and plays, novels, myths, fairy tales, even jokes). The first act typically depicts "life as normal" for the protagonist. In the second act, the protagonist must leave his normal life and battle the antagonist for what he (the protagonist) wants. After the battle, which may be real or metaphoric, the protagonist sees his goal in reach, and in the third act the protagonist goes for it, carrying out his plan and suc- ceeding or failing as the story resolves itself.

Act I break   The boundary between the first and second acts. The break is usually marked by an event that takes the story off in a new—often surprising or unexpected—direction. As a story detective, you found that event in Chapter 13, when the hero could no longer ignore the problem that kept popping up in his life.

Midpoint   The event in the middle of the second act (and therefore the middle of the script) when the protagonist commits to solving his prob- lem or going after what he wants. Prior to the midpoint, the protagonist had the (sometimes painful) option of returning to his old life and giving up his quest, struggle, or journey. After the midpoint, that door is closed. As a story detective, you found the midpoint moment in Chapter 15.

All-is-lost moment   At some point in the latter half of the second act, the protagonist encounters a situation in which it appears he can't over- come the odds against him, and any chance of success is illusionary. As a story detective, you found this moment at the end of Chapter 15.

Act II break   The boundary between the second and third acts is marked by the point where the protagonist figures out a way out of his predicament. The realization doesn't ensure the protagonist is going to prevail, only that he has moved from a position of no hope to one of "just maybe …." In your story detective work, you found this moment in Chapter 16.

Want   A want is what the protagonist … well … *wants*. It's typically the reason for and the driving force behind the story. This book uses the term *problem* for want because, most of the time, having the want manifests itself as a problem for the protagonist. Often, writers mistakenly treat wants as internal feelings—the protagonist wants to be happy—which creates difficulties when you try to turn that want into a film. We can see whether the protagonist solves his problem. Just what does "wants to be happy" look like on the screen?

Resolution   This term refers to most of what happens in the final act, although you can also view the resolution as the specific moment in which the audience learns whether and how the protagonist does or doesn't solve his problem.

Need   Often, the protagonist *needs* to learn something to move the story along. This isn't learning in the book sense. It's learning in the human sense. The protagonist may need to learn to be less of a jerk or more assertive or more like a mentor or parent. In this case, you'll hear your tale described as a need-driven story.

HOW DO I KNOW WHEN IT'S TIME TO MOVE FROM OUTLINE TO SCRIPT?

When you ask yourself this question, congratulations. It's time to take off your story detective's trench coat and reveal your screenwriter's clothes.

Sample Final Report

Under a banner that says "Career Day 1971," a prim, proper, and unimaginatively dressed Francine stands in front of her nephew Stanley's elementary school classmates. With all the enthusiasm she can muster—and for Francine, that's a formidable amount—she extols the virtues of working at the post office and the excitement of punching the first 3 digits of ZIP codes into a letter sorting machine for hours on end. Throughout the auditorium, kids fidget, talk, and use ballpoint pens to etch their initials into the wooden arms of their seats. As Francine continues, undaunted, we see Stanley sitting in the far corner of the auditorium, burying his face in his hands.

At 58, Francine feels time is her enemy. Every week she works out, watches her diet, and tries to rekindle the spark of youthful romance with her husband, Horace. But since embarrassing her nephew, Stanley, while speaking at his school's career day, Francine has been obsessed with writing a book. Vowing to give Stanley a relative he can be proud of, she works on her book constantly, much to the consternation of her friends, associates, and strangers, who find her making notes, dictating into her voice recorder, and asking them strange—and mostly annoying—questions quite irritating. But Francine, it is her last chance to, as she put it, accomplish something she could be proud of.

Taking a break from book authorship, Francine heads to Idaho to visit Stanley and takes her nephew to the county fair. Demonstrating her youthfulness, she matches Stanley corn dog for corn dog, cotton candy for cotton candy, and scary ride for scary ride. It is after the Tilt-a-Whirl, though, that the spinning scenery, flashing lights, and random diet finally claim her as a victim. Exiting the ride, Francine stumbles, spins around, and, before falling to the ground, leaves the vivid, yellow-green tinged details of everything she's eaten all over the midway lawn.

Back home the next day, and despite her doctor's orders, Francine goes for her usual morning run. Not only does she double-time it, she makes a point of telling virtually everyone she passes—nearly a dozen startled runners and twice as many passers-by—that she is in the best shape ever.

For the next few weeks, Francine seems to shut herself off from the rest of the world. She works longer and longer hours. She no longer meets Horace at the door with a glass of her special lemonade when he returns from blowing up canned vegetables in the woods near their home. Horace jokes that he doesn't have a wife and begins calling Francine his "boarder." Oblivious, Francine cranks out page after page of her book as if racing some competing, imaginary author toward an equally imaginary finish line.

Francine takes a short leave of absence from the post office in order to pound out her book without distractions. Many months—and several emergency home and car repairs later—Horace and Francine are nearly out of money. When the bank notifies them their mortgage is in default, Francine meets with the manager to reason with him. One word leads to another, and Francine throws a temper tantrum right in the middle of the bank. Nobody knows what to do. The customers all turn away and ignore her. The guard, an unarmed kid who doesn't seem to know if it is okay to physically restrain a female customer, is helpless. Eventually, everyone is relieved when Francine storms out.

Carla's offhand comment that Francine should return to the post office or start robbing banks is all the encouragement she needs. A few days later, heavily disguised and wrapped in a fur coat, Francine walks into the crowded bank. She quietly places a small package next to a potted plant and waits in an agonizingly slow line for a teller. In front of the teller, Francine opens her coat to reveal she is stark naked. People gasp. Mothers cover their children's eyes. Men stare as their wives hit them over the head with shopping bags. Francine demands all the money to cover herself back up. As before, nobody knows quite what to do. Suddenly, and somewhat prematurely, a loud bang comes from the vicinity of the potted plant, and creamed corn spews everywhere. An angry and empty-handed Francine darts out the back door. When the police arrive on the scene, all the witnesses can agree on, at least the male witnesses, is that she had <u>some</u> body.

Word of the strange doings in the bank generate buzz, and shortly thereafter, the owner of the gallery where Horace has a few of his paintings on consignment calls. Horace's work sold out, at excellent prices. Could he and Francine come to New York City? A reporter for the <u>Times</u> wants to do a story on him. And how quickly can he make more art?

After a successful trip to New York, Horace and Francine return home with enough money to forestall the foreclosure and allow Francine to return to her writing. When Francine describes the trip to Carla, Carla observes that Francine didn't seem as happy as she should be about this turn of events.

As the incident in the bank fades from view, so does Horace's art sales. The gallery stops calling. Likewise, the reporters. Francine does the only thing she can think of. She puts on another disguise, her fur coat, and nothing else, and explodes another can of vegetables in another bank. Creamed spinach this time. Although she demands cash to cover up, she makes no attempt to take the money. In no time, Horace's art is back in high demand.

Francine feels she is losing her husband. In between working around the clock on his art, Horace travels to New York to make the round of celebrity parties where he seems to pay attention to everyone but her. At one soirée, he is fawned over by all manner of celebrities, including Arnold, the pig from <u>Green Acres</u>.

Horace also announces that the person he'd most like to meet is the mystery woman who explodes the cans of vegetables in banks. He calls her a kindred spirit, and says that her performance art is making a wonderful statement. To Francine, that is akin to her husband running off with another woman.

After a few more bank "performances," Francine can't take it any longer. She hates how Horace fawns over her alter ego. She hates even more that he seems so romantically disengaged from her. One evening, just before bed, she comes out of the bathroom dressed in her fur coat and nothing else, snuggles up to him, and asks how he'd like to make some real explosions with his mystery muse.

Francine and Horace make passionate love. In the afterglow, Francine anticipates cuddling close to her wonderful husband, after confessing to him about her double life. Horace misses the confession part completely, assuming Francine is helping him live out his fantasy of sex with his muse. Saying they "have words" doesn't do justice to the situation, which is best summed up by Horace's sleeping on the living room couch.

The next morning, Francine marches into the middle of the busy squad room and in a loud voice, confesses to being the mystery bank robber. When the detectives on duty hardly notice, Francine opens her coat and stands there naked. After a careful discussion among the police, who rely on the expert opinion of a couple prostitutes on their way to the courthouse, all present conclude it isn't her. The real mystery woman is considerably younger, with rounder breasts and a firmer tummy. Francine is held in custody, for her own protection, until Horace can take her home.

In the aftermath, Horace fears Francine is having a breakdown. Joan is furious Francine would lie just to make herself look important to Stanley. And when Stanley finds out Horace has met Arnold the pig, he invites Horace, not Francine, to speak at career day. Joan insists Horace come without the pig ... and without Francine.

Francine secretly travels to visit Stanley at career day, intent on confessing that she tried to make him proud, pretending not to be insignificant. It's just that they come from a long line of insignificant people. Not wanting to be caught and create a scene, Francine sneaks into the school and ducks into a classroom, only to find it is being used by parents and students to prepare cookies and lemonade for the event. It is the worst lemonade she has ever tasted. Proclaiming she would never let her husband drink that awful stuff, she proceeds to show the kids how to make lemonade properly. It is a huge hit, and Francine credits the recipe to her brilliant nephew, Stanley.

Back home and snuggling in bed, Horace and Francine watch an 11 o'clock news report of the police arresting a suspect who claims to be the mystery woman behind the explosions of canned vegetables in banks. The police are convinced the woman is the perpetrator because she has a history of unstable behavior. Francine laughs. Horace sighs. They both roll closer to each other, and Horace turns off the light.

Flash forward 20 years. At a small graveside ceremony, Francine's body is laid to rest alongside her dearly departed Horace. The officiating priest makes some comments about how in love and devoted they were to each other in their final years. Carla, in a wheelchair, sobs softly. Joan seeks support on Stanley's shoulder. Stanley has grown up to become a fine-looking man, and he is well dressed in an expensive black suit.

After the ceremony, Stanley and Joan climb into a limo and are whisked to the airport, where they board a private jet. As the plane speeds down the runway, the words "Aunt Fran's Fruit Drinks, Inc." on the side of the fuselage fly by. As the plane lifts off, the setting sun glints off the company's logo, a sketch of Francine's face, emblazoned on the plane's tail.

Index

D

E

F–G

H

I–J–K

R

S

T–U

V

W–X–Y–Z